© Stonewell Healing Press, 2025
All rights reserved.

This book is a labor of care. Please do not copy, share, or distribute any part of it—digitally or physically—without written permission from the author or publisher, except for brief excerpts used in reviews or critical articles. Your respect helps this work reach others who need it.

This workbook is not a replacement for therapy, crisis support, or mental health treatment. It's meant to offer reflection, comfort, and growth—not clinical care. If you're struggling, please reach out to a licensed professional. You matter too much to go through it alone.

Every effort has been made to ensure this content is accurate, responsible, and thoughtful. The author and publisher cannot guarantee outcomes and are not liable for misuse or misinterpretation of the material.

Thank you for being here. We're honored to walk beside you.

M. Tourangeau
Stonewell Healing Press

TABLE OF CONTENTS

SECTION 1 -   **1**

The Hidden Trauma of In-Law Relationships

SECTION 2 -   **27**

The Cost of Keeping the Peace

SECTION 3 -   **51**

Gaslighting, Guilt, and Good Intentions

SECTION 4 -   **77**

Your Nervous System Knows

SECTION 5 -   **101**

When Your Partner Doesn't See It

SECTION 6   **129**

Emotional Puppeteering – Guilt Trips, Gifts with Strings, and Control Disguised as Care

Stonewell Healing Press

TABLE OF CONTENTS

SECTION 7 -   **157**

When Kids Are Involved – Protecting Your Children from Toxic Dynamics Without Losing Yourself

---

SECTION 8-   **181**

The Partner Problem – When They Don't See It, Don't Believe You, or Don't Want to Rock the Boat

---

SECTION 9 -   **207**

When You Have Kids – Protecting Their Peace Without Inheriting the Dysfunction

---

SECTION 10 -   **233**

Reclaiming Your Inner Authority

SECTION 11 -   **255**

Staying, Leaving, or Going Low Contact – Choosing Peace Over Obligation

---

SECTION 12 -   **275**

Parenting in the Eye of the Storm

TABLE OF CONTENTS

SECTION 13 -   **297**

Letting Go of the Fantasy – Grieving the Relationship You Wished They Could Be

---

SECTION 14-   **319**

Staying, Leaving, or Detaching – Making the Right Choice for You

---

CLOSING   **338**

When You Have Kids – Protecting Their Peace Without Inheriting the Dysfunction

Dedicated to those who fought to
feel accepted, respected, and loved
by their bonus family.

STONEWELL HEALING PRESS

HOW TO USE THIS WORKBOOK

Take your time with this. The more you pause to really think about each question and answer honestly, the more space you create for reflection. And with deeper reflection, this experience can open up new understanding and healing you might not expect.

Be honest with yourself—there's no judgment here. This is your private space. If you want, you can even throw this book away or burn it later to keep your secrets safe. That said, be mindful of how much you dive in. Healing and reflection around tough, sensitive topics can bring up strong feelings—and yes, it can get triggering. So here's your gentle trigger warning.

The real progress comes when you practice the skills, not just read about them. The more you try them out in your life, the more helpful this workbook will be.

11

STONEWELL HEALING PRESS

ASSESSMENT

WHERE AM I NOW?

Before we begin, take a moment to honestly check in with yourself by rating these statements on a scale from 1 (not at all) to 10 (completely):

1-10

1. I trust my own perception, even when others try to twist or dismiss my reality.

2. I can set boundaries without being swallowed by guilt, fear, or shame.

3. I value my own peace more than avoiding conflict or keeping others comfortable.

4. I can recognize gaslighting in the moment and hold onto my clarity instead of collapsing into confusion.

5. I notice how stress shows up in my body and respond with care instead of ignoring or pushing through.

6. When my needs or boundaries are dismissed, I can respond in a way that protects my dignity and self-respect.

7. I can sit with hard emotions—anger, grief, fear—without shutting down, exploding, or abandoning myself.

8. When I picture my future relationships, I imagine myself safe, respected, and fully present as my whole self.

SECTION ONE

The Hidden Trauma of In-Law Relationships

It's one of the deepest, most confusing emotional wounds: when the people who are supposed to "become family" instead become a source of chronic pain, disrespect, or fear. You may have tried everything — being kind, keeping the peace, setting boundaries, explaining yourself — and still found yourself walking on eggshells or questioning your own sanity. Maybe others don't see it. Maybe your partner doesn't fully get it. Maybe you've even wondered if you are the problem. You're not.

This kind of relational harm often goes unrecognized — but it's real. And it's traumatic. It erodes your sense of safety, dignity, and belonging, especially when it happens inside a family system you're supposed to merge with. Whether the damage is overt or subtle, loud or quiet, intentional or unconscious, it matters because it hurts you. And here, finally, is a space where that pain will be named, held, and healed — without minimizing, gaslighting, or guilt.

Making Sense Of It
Why In-Law Trauma Cuts So Deep

When most people hear the word "trauma," they think of the obvious: car accidents, natural disasters, physical violence. What they don't think of are the quiet dinner tables where every word feels like walking through a minefield. They don't picture holidays where you paste on a smile while your insides twist. They don't imagine the in-law who dominates every conversation under the disguise of "just being honest." But here's the truth: trauma isn't measured by how dramatic something looks on the outside. It's measured by what it does to your nervous system, your sense of self, and your core feeling of safety in the world.

When your needs are minimized, your boundaries crossed, or your truth consistently dismissed — especially inside systems that expect you to "be grateful" or "keep the family peace" — it doesn't just sting. It chips away at identity. This is what psychologists call chronic relational trauma: not one catastrophic event, but the repeated erosion of safety and worth inside the very relationships where love and belonging are supposed to live.

Polyvagal theory tells us our nervous system is wired to seek safety through connection. We are biologically designed to calm down when we feel seen, heard, and understood. But when the very people who should provide that safety instead become a source of fear, manipulation, or constant criticism, the body flips into survival mode. That can mean fight (arguing to be heard), flight (avoiding calls, visits, or hard conversations), freeze (going numb just to get through it), or fawn (people-pleasing to stay safe). Over time, these survival strategies become so ingrained that they feel like personality traits rather than protective reflexes.

Making Sense Of It
Why In-Law Trauma Cuts So Deep

And there's another layer: culture and family roles. In many families, conflict-avoidance, deference to elders, or sacrificing your truth for harmony isn't just tolerated — it's expected. Anthropologists have long noted that families function like micro-cultures, with rules, hierarchies, and roles that can be hard to break. Maybe you've been assigned the role of peacemaker, scapegoat, or "good daughter/son-in-law." Maybe you've learned to swallow your truth just to keep the system running smoothly. On the outside, it looks like cooperation. On the inside, it feels like suffocation.

That's why this pain cuts so deep: it's not just about one person's words or actions. It's about the clash between your nervous system's need for safety, your culture's unspoken rules about loyalty and harmony, and your own longing to be seen as you are. You're not "too sensitive." You're not overreacting. You are responding exactly as a human body and heart respond when belonging turns dangerous.

This workbook is about breaking that cycle. Through trauma-informed care, nervous system integration, and inner parts work (like Internal Family Systems), you'll learn to name the unseen wounds, release the shame of "why does this bother me so much," and reclaim the safety that was always your birthright. Your pain is not only valid — it is survivable. And in time, it can become the very doorway to your deepest resilience.

What hurts the most — and what are you not allowed to say out loud?

We often minimize our own pain before anyone else has to. What have you silenced to keep the peace? What words feel dangerous or "too much" to say, even inside your own head? Let this page be a space where nothing has to be polished, justified, or made palatable. What's the raw, unsaid truth?

What hurts the most — and what are you not allowed to say out loud?

What would it feel like to believe that your pain is real — without apology?

Imagine someone you trust looking you in the eye and saying, "You're not imagining this. It's real." What happens in your body when you picture that? What part of you feels relief? What part feels disbelief? Let both speak here.

What would it feel like to believe that your pain is real — without apology?

What roles have you unconsciously taken on to survive in-law dynamics?

Have you become the fixer, the appeaser, the invisible one, the one who makes jokes to defuse tension? Reflect gently on the personas you've adopted to avoid conflict — and whether those parts are tired, resentful, or ready to be seen.

What roles have you unconsciously taken on to survive in-law dynamics?

How has this impacted your relationship with your partner — or with yourself?

Toxic in-law dynamics don't just stay in one corner of your life. How has this stress shown up in your relationship, your body, your ability to rest or feel safe? How much of yourself have you had to hide?

How has this impacted your relationship with your partner — or with yourself?

Who do you become around them — and who do you wish you could be instead?

Write about the shift you notice in yourself when you're near or even thinking about them. Do you shrink, tense up, overperform? What would it feel like to stay regulated, honest, and grounded — no matter who's in the room?

Who do you become around them — and who do you wish you could be instead?

What part of you still hopes they'll change — and what does that part need instead?

Hope is powerful, but it can also keep us stuck. Get curious: is there a younger part of you holding onto hope that someday they'll see you, love you, apologize? What would it feel like to grieve that — without shame?

What part of you still hopes they'll change — and what does that part need instead?

What do you wish someone else — anyone — would say to you about this?

Whether it's validation, permission, protection, or just someone finally believing you, write the words you most long to hear. Then consider: can you begin saying them to yourself?

What do you wish someone else — anyone — would say to you about this?

TRACING THE TRUTH

THE SAFETY CLASH

Families often assign us roles that we play to keep the system stable: peacemaker, scapegoat, caretaker, silent one, conflict-avoider. But those roles don't always match our authentic self. In the table below, write down the roles you've been expected to play in your family, then explore what those roles cost you, and what the real you actually needs.

Why it helps:
This exercise makes visible the clash between your biology (nervous system safety) and your social/familial expectations. Seeing that gap in black and white reduces self-blame — it shows you're not broken, you're navigating an impossible double bind.

In the first circle, write what your body truly needs to feel safe (e.g., respect, honesty, calm tone, space).
In the second circle, write what your family expects to "keep the peace" (e.g., silence, agreement, avoiding conflict).
In the overlapping middle, add anything the two have in common — if there is overlap at all.

Step back and notice: How much overlap is there? Where do your needs and your family's rules clash?

TRACING THE TRUTH

THE SAFETY CLASH

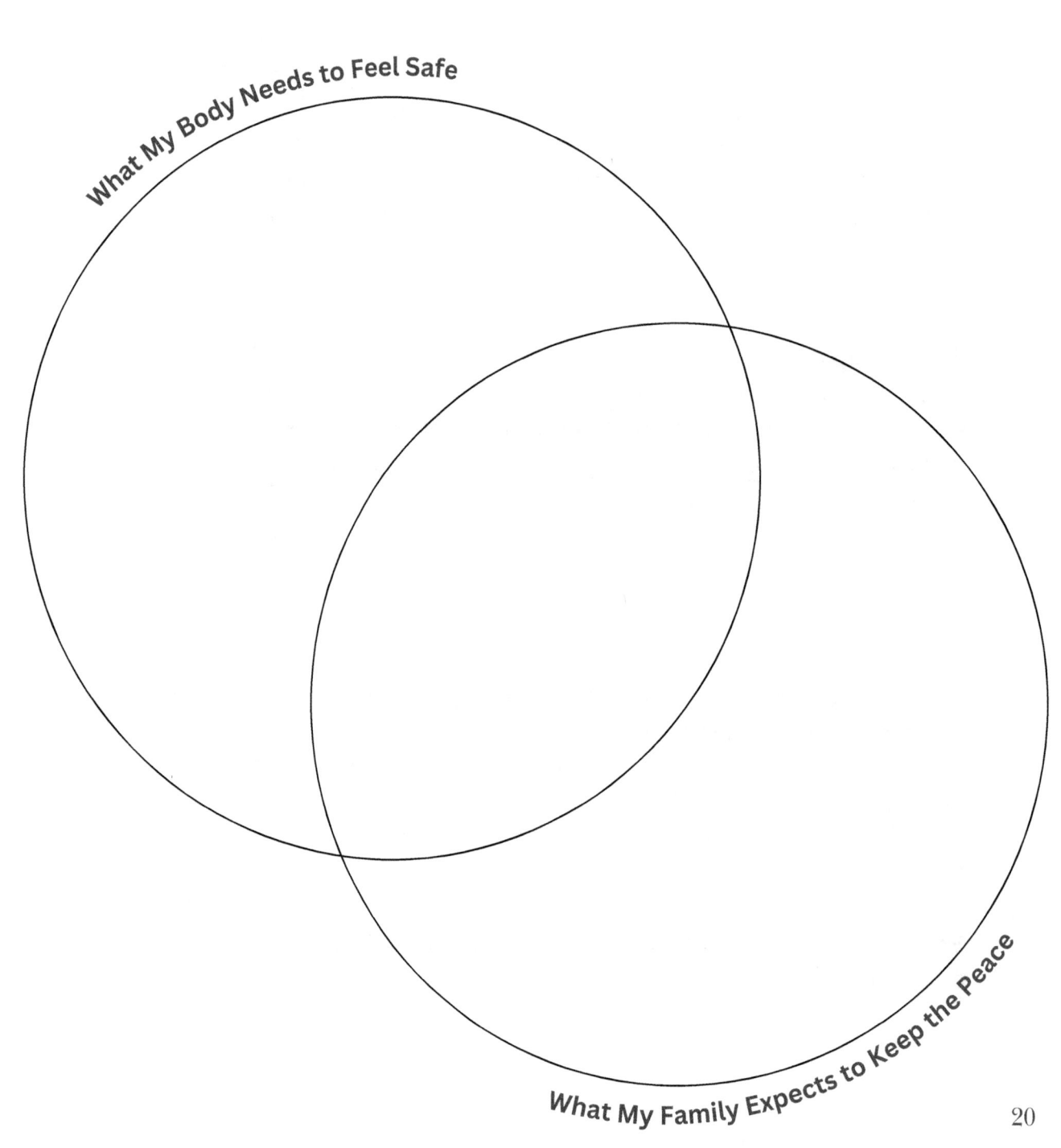

20

TRACING THE TRUTH

THE ROLE VS. THE REAL ME

Families often assign us roles that we play to keep the system stable: peacemaker, scapegoat, caretaker, silent one, conflict-avoider. But those roles don't always match our authentic self. In the table below, write down the roles you've been expected to play in your family, then explore what those roles cost you, and what the real you actually needs.

Why it helps:
This exercise helps you externalize the "roles" (which are cultural/familial constructs, not who you truly are) and reclaim your deeper self that exists beneath them.

Family Role I've Played	What It Cost Me	What the Real Me Needs

TRACING THE TRUTH

THE ROLE VS. THE REAL ME

Family Role I've Played	What It Cost Me	What the Real Me Needs

EMERGENCY TOOL

If You're Activated Right Now...

f just reading this section made your heart race, your stomach drop, or your mind go blank — pause here. Your body is telling you something important. You're safe now, and you don't have to push through. Try this:
Orient to the room. Look around and name five neutral objects out loud. "There's a lamp. A window. A book. A plant. A cup."

Touch something cool or textured. Run your fingers over a surface. Notice the sensation fully.

Say this out loud or write it down:

"I am not there. I am here. I have choices now. I am not alone in this."

Place your hand on your heart. Feel the weight of it. Breathe.

Come back to the workbook when you feel steadier. This is your healing — you get to go at your pace.

MAPPING YOUR RESILIENCE

When life is painful, the spotlight lands on what's broken or lost. But every hard season you've lived through also carries evidence of your resilience. Mapping your past with a "strength lens" helps you reclaim those forgotten skills — endurance, creativity, boundary-setting, persistence, humor, or compassion. Trauma research shows that naming and revisiting these strengths rebuilds self-trust. Instead of seeing your past only as a string of wounds, you begin to recognize the ways you showed up for yourself. Circling three core strengths creates a personal toolkit you can consciously bring forward into your next chapter.

1. **Draw Your Timeline** —Mark a few "hard seasons" you've lived through on the timeline.

2. **Name Strengths** — Under each event, write one or two strengths you used to get through (e.g., courage, asking for help, persistence).

3. **Circle Three** — Look at the whole map. Circle three strengths that feel most alive, relevant, or needed for where you're headed now.

4. **Carry Them Forward** — Write them on a sticky note or card where you'll see them often — reminders that you've done hard things before, and you will again.

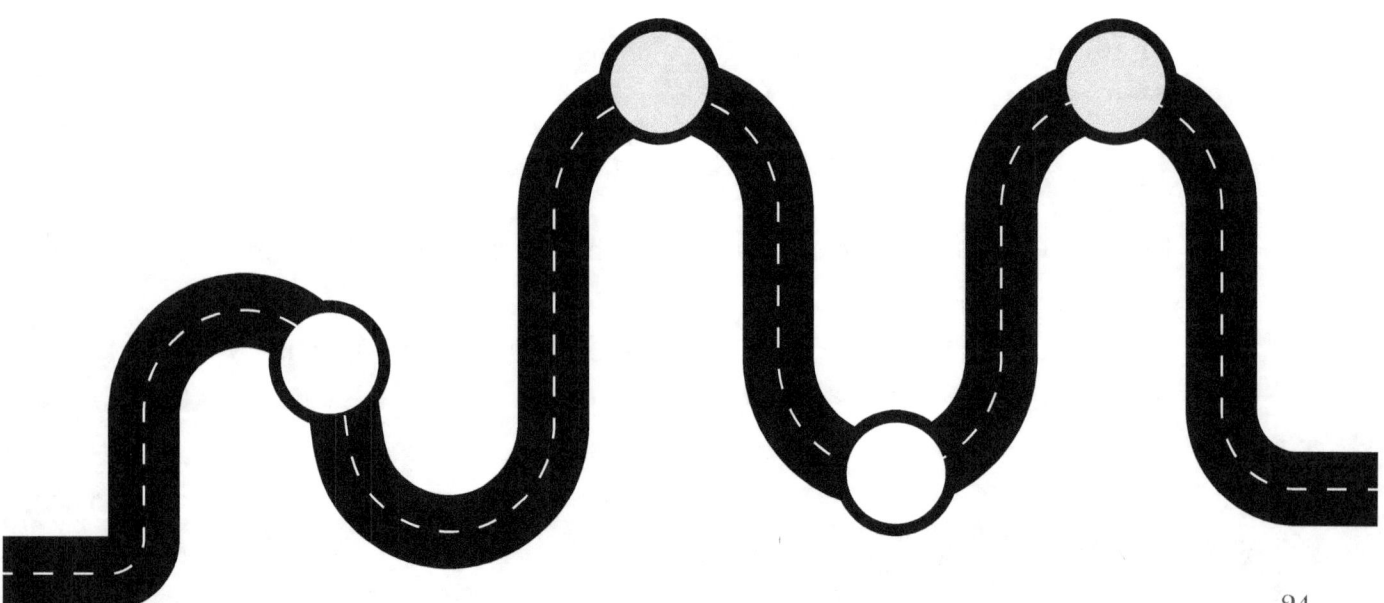

SAFE/BRAVE COLLAGE

Healing doesn't mean throwing yourself into the deep end. It means finding the edges of your current safety and gently stretching them. This exercise blends comfort and courage, showing your nervous system that bravery doesn't have to mean danger. Visual imagery (like collage) activates deeper parts of the brain than words alone, helping you bypass self-criticism and connect with possibility. Placing one "brave" image inside your "safe" space signals: I can grow without abandoning myself. This balance between grounding and stretching is key for trauma recovery, resilience, and lasting change.

Collect Images — Use magazines, printouts, or sketches. On the Safe side, paste images that represent rest, comfort, and security. On the Brave side, add images that symbolize courage, growth, or edges you dream of touching.

The Bridge Step — Choose one tiny image of bravery and place it into the Safe half. This represents your next gentle edge — a stretch that doesn't abandon your grounding.

Reflect — Ask yourself: What's one small way I can practice this edge this wee

SAFE	BRAVE

SECTION TWO

The Cost of Keeping the Peace

Sometimes, peace isn't peace — it's performance under pressure. It's the forced smile, the choked-down truth, the thousand quiet betrayals of self just to avoid another argument, another cold shoulder, another guilt trip. In-law dynamics can make you feel like your only job is to "not make waves," even if it means swallowing your own pain. You may have heard: "Don't be dramatic," "Let it go," "They didn't mean it." And so you stayed quiet. You softened your tone. You turned the other cheek — over and over again.

But silence isn't the same as peace. And being "the bigger person" doesn't work if it's just another word for disappearing. The truth is, you can't keep peace if it keeps costing your dignity, your mental health, or your voice. In this section, we'll unpack what it really means to "keep the peace" — and what it's already cost you — so you can begin reclaiming your inner ground, without guilt.

Making Sense Of It
The Hidden Cost of "Keeping the Peace"

When people imagine survival instincts, they usually think of fight or flight. But trauma psychology has identified another, often hidden, response: the fawn response. Fawning doesn't look like escape or confrontation — it looks like appeasing, smoothing over, or making yourself smaller so that conflict never fully erupts. From the outside, it may look like being "easygoing" or "selfless." On the inside, it's your nervous system doing whatever it takes to stay safe.

This is especially common in family systems where asserting your needs leads to ridicule, punishment, or rejection. Anthropologists often describe families as small-scale cultures with their own rules and hierarchies. In some, there's an unspoken contract: loyalty and silence are valued above individuality. In these environments, fawning isn't a choice; it's a reflexive strategy to preserve belonging. But belonging at the cost of self eventually becomes suffocating.

Over time, living in fawn mode blurs the line between who you are and who you've had to be. It chips away at authenticity and replaces it with exhaustion, resentment, and disconnection. Many describe feeling anxious, panicked, or hollow — as if their truth is buried beneath layers of compliance. And yet, the fawn response is not weakness. It is survival. It is your body's best attempt to keep you connected in environments where connection felt conditional.

Making Sense Of It
The Hidden Cost of "Keeping the Peace"

There's also a societal layer here. In many cultures, especially those with strong emphasis on family honor or collective harmony, "keeping the peace" is praised while healthy conflict is punished. Women, in particular, are often socialized to absorb discomfort, manage others' emotions, and make themselves smaller to maintain harmony. Men may be told that their worth lies in being "easygoing" or "unbothered." These cultural scripts reinforce the fawn response and make it harder to recognize it as survival rather than personality.

Neuroscience helps explain why this runs so deep. The nervous system is wired to prioritize safety over authenticity. When it perceives risk — a raised voice, a cold withdrawal, a subtle criticism — it will sacrifice self-expression to preserve attachment. In childhood, this reflex can be lifesaving. In adulthood, it can quietly erode intimacy, autonomy, and self-trust. That's why so many people who fawn end up asking, "Why don't I know what I want anymore?" or "Why do I feel invisible even in my closest relationships?"

Healing begins with noticing. Recognizing that "keeping the peace" isn't a flaw in your character but a nervous system adaptation is a turning point. From there, the work is gradual: honoring the part of you that fawned to survive, and gently allowing other parts — the boundary-setter, the truth-teller, the self-protector — to return. Each time you risk being real instead of pleasing, you remind your body that safety and authenticity can coexist. And with each step, you reclaim not just your voice, but your wholeness.

What have you done — or not done — in the name of "keeping the peace"?

List the ways you've censored yourself, stayed silent, made excuses, or tolerated mistreatment in order to keep family dynamics stable. Let yourself be honest, even if it's painful. You're not blaming yourself — you're naming the cost.

What have you done — or not done — in the name of "keeping the peace"?

Who benefits when you stay silent? And who suffers?

Think about how the power dynamics shift when you suppress your truth. Who remains comfortable, unchallenged, or dominant? And what does your silence cost you — emotionally, physically, or spiritually?

Who benefits when you stay silent? And who suffers?

When you've tried to assert yourself, what happened?

Reflect on moments when you did speak up. Were you ignored, blamed, mocked, guilted, or retaliated against? Writing this down helps validate the survival intelligence behind your silence — and explore whether the cost of it is still worth it.

When you've tried to assert yourself, what happened?

What messages did you grow up with around "being the bigger person"?

Did your family teach you that forgiveness means forgetting? That good people don't get angry? That rocking the boat is selfish or shameful? Unpacking these messages helps you reclaim your right to wholeness.

What messages did you grow up with around "being the bigger person"?

How do you feel in your body before, during, and after conflict avoidance?

Get curious: When you avoid confrontation, does your body tighten or go numb? Does your chest clench or your heart race? Let your body teach you how much energy goes into peacekeeping.

How do you feel in your body before, during, and after conflict avoidance?

What are you afraid will happen if you stop trying to keep the peace?

Be radically honest here. Are you afraid of rejection, judgment, abandonment, losing your partner's approval, or being blamed? What part of you is trying to protect you from that pain?

What are you afraid will happen if you stop trying to keep the peace?

What would a more honest version of "peace" look like for you?

Imagine a peace that includes you — where you feel safe, respected, and not responsible for everyone else's comfort. What boundaries, truths, or shifts would that kind of peace require?

What would a more honest version of "peace" look like for you?

TRACING THE TRUTH

THE INNER COST LEDGER

Fawning often convinces us that keeping the peace protects everyone — that if we can just absorb the discomfort, everything will stay intact. But what's rarely acknowledged is the quiet, personal cost of carrying that role. This exercise helps you hold both truths at once: what your efforts have preserved, and what they've taken from you. By putting them side by side, you begin to see the hidden math of survival that your nervous system has been running for years.

Why it helps:
This can help you interrupt the cycle of self-doubt and emotional hijacking. By gently and clearly name the emotional, physical, and relational toll that conflict avoidance has taken on you over time.

In the "protected" column, list all the things you've shielded through peacekeeping — your partner's comfort, the illusion of harmony, the family dynamic, the kids' stability, etc.

Now, in the "cost" column, name what you've sacrificed: your voice, sleep, confidence, energy, trust, clarity, peace of mind. Be honest.

Step back and look. Let this visual become a mirror. Are the protections worth the price?

TRACING THE TRUTH

THE INNER COST LEDGER

What I've Protected	What It's Cost Me

TINY WINS PROTOCOL

When you're overwhelmed, your brain can trick you into believing nothing is possible. Big goals feel impossible, so you stall. But tiny actions build proof: I can move. Completing a single small task sparks dopamine — the brain's reward chemical — and that fuels momentum. Instead of waiting for motivation, you create it by acting first. Two-minute wins keep you out of the freeze state and remind you that forward movement doesn't need to be dramatic to matter. Over time, stacking these little completions can shift your entire day — and even your sense of self. It's not about doing everything; it's about proving to yourself that you can do something.

Pick a micro-task: Something that takes under 2 minutes (wash mug, text back, stretch, shower).

02 Countdown launch: Mental health awareness helps reduce stigma, promotes empathy, and encourages open conversations about mental health concerns.

03 Complete & log: Write it down or check it off for a small hit of satisfaction.

04 Notice momentum: Let the success energy carry you into the next doable action.

05 Repeat daily: Build trust with yourself through small, steady proof points.

ACTION

THREE PILLARS BEFORE NOON

When you're caught in anxiety, depression, or burnout, your nervous system can swing between shutdown and overdrive. The quickest way to steady yourself is to touch three key areas: body, mind, and pleasure. Moving your body brings energy online; completing a mastery task (even something small like an email) restores a sense of competence; and engaging in pleasure reminds you that joy and safety are still accessible. This "trio" isn't about being productive — it's about balance. Think of it as a daily reset button. By noon, if you've already touched your body, completed one mastery task, and tasted one moment of pleasure, you've laid down anchors for resilience. Instead of asking your day to be perfect, you give yourself three touchpoints that prove: I can show up, I can accomplish, and I can enjoy.

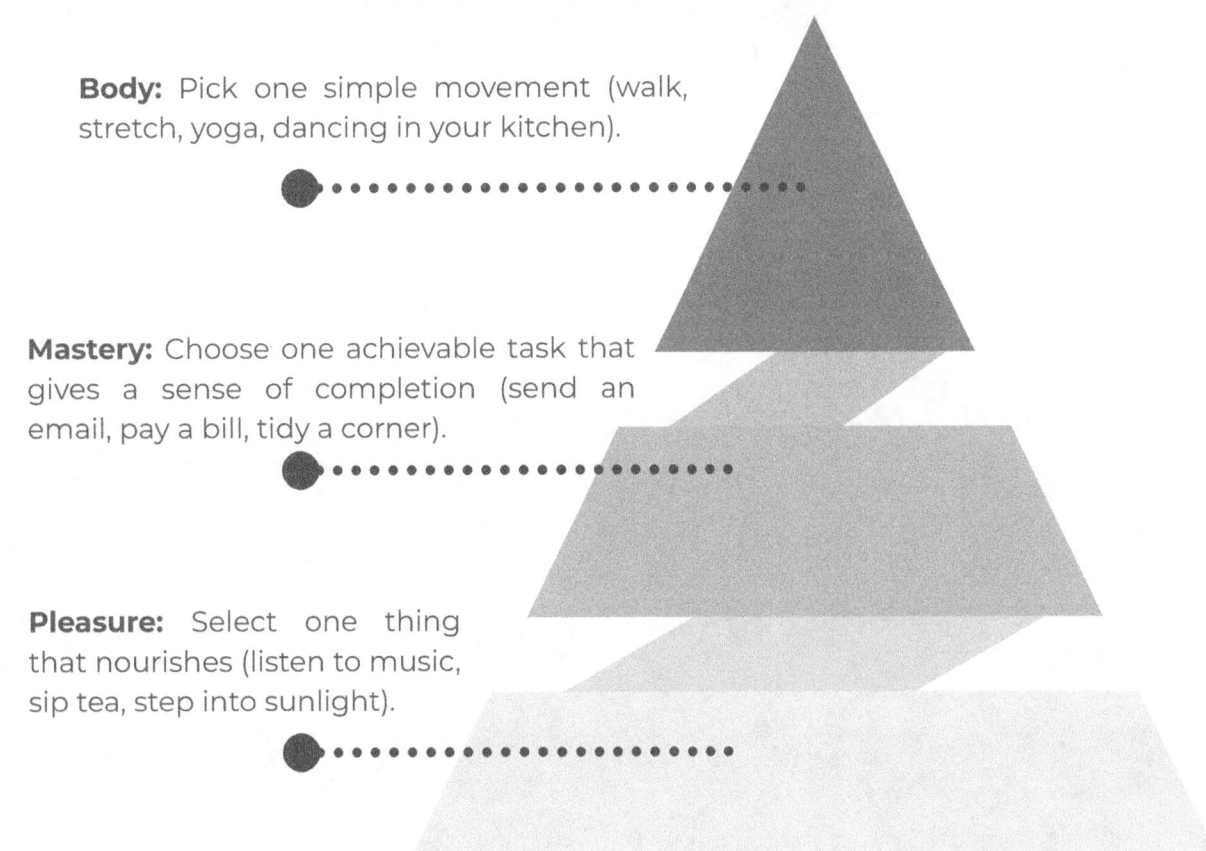

Body: Pick one simple movement (walk, stretch, yoga, dancing in your kitchen).

Mastery: Choose one achievable task that gives a sense of completion (send an email, pay a bill, tidy a corner).

Pleasure: Select one thing that nourishes (listen to music, sip tea, step into sunlight).

Stack them early: Aim to complete all three before noon to set your rhythm.

Reflect briefly: Notice how touching all three domains shifts your mood and energy.

SECTION THREE

Gaslighting, Guilt, and Good Intentions

Some of the deepest harm doesn't come from direct cruelty — it comes from confusing kindness. From words that sound sweet but feel sharp. From "I'm only trying to help" that leaves you hollow. From "You're too sensitive" when you're just reacting to something real. Gaslighting and guilt don't always scream — sometimes they smile. And that makes them even harder to name, let alone confront.

You might have been told you were overreacting, imagining things, misremembering, or too emotional. You may have started to question your instincts, your memory, even your grip on reality. That's not an accident — it's the emotional impact of psychological manipulation. And whether it's intentional or unconscious, the damage is the same: it disconnects you from your own truth. In this section, we'll untangle the tactics that have kept you stuck in shame or self-doubt — and start helping you reclaim your clarity, your voice, and your reality.

Making Sense Of It
Gaslighting: Why It Shakes You to the Core

Gaslighting isn't just a buzzword — it's a systematic dismantling of trust in yourself. At its heart, gaslighting makes you question whether you can rely on your own perception, memory, or emotions. When someone rewrites reality in front of you — and insists you accept their version — it strikes at the foundation of your identity. Because what are we, if not our ability to notice, remember, and make sense of our own lives?

In in-law dynamics, gaslighting often hides behind cultural scripts like "respect," "tradition," or "keeping the family together." It might sound like:

- "That never happened — you're remembering it wrong."
- "You always take things the wrong way."
- "We were just joking. Don't be so sensitive."
- "We're only trying to help — you should be grateful."

On the surface, these phrases may appear trivial, even laughable. But repeated over time, they create a slow erosion of self-trust. You start editing yourself before you even speak. You wonder, Am I the problem? Maybe it wasn't that bad. Maybe I am too much. That internal second-guessing is the deeper damage of gaslighting: you begin doing the work of silencing yourself, even when no one else is in the room.

Making Sense Of It
Gaslighting: Why It Shakes You to the Core

From a psychological perspective, gaslighting exploits a deep human need for belonging. Social psychology and anthropology both remind us that humans are wired to survive in groups; historically, exile from the tribe meant danger, even death. So when a family system — especially one you've married into — pressures you to conform to its version of reality, your nervous system often goes along, even when it hurts. Conformity feels safer than conflict. This is why so many people trapped in gaslighting dynamics ask themselves later, Why didn't I speak up sooner? The answer isn't weakness — it's biology.

But biology isn't destiny. According to Dialectical Behavior Therapy (DBT), the antidote to chronic invalidation is radical self-trust and emotional mindfulness. You don't need anyone else's permission to know what you felt. You don't need the people who hurt you to confirm that it happened. Reclaiming your reality starts with pausing when doubt creeps in and asking: What do I know to be true in my body, in my memory, in my heart?

Healing from gaslighting is less about "winning" against the person who distorted you and more about stopping the cycle of self-gaslighting inside your own mind. That means practicing micro-moments of trust: writing down what happened before someone convinces you otherwise, naming your feelings without apology, and remembering that your truth deserves space — even if no one else in the room agrees.

What moments come to mind when you've questioned your own reality?

Describe a time you left a conversation or visit feeling small, confused, or unsure of what just happened. What did you feel in your gut — and how did your mind try to talk you out of it?

What moments come to mind when you've questioned your own reality?

What phrases do they use that seem kind on the surface — but feel off?

Write down any "nice" language that doesn't land as loving: "We're just trying to help," "Don't be like that," "You're imagining things." How do these words impact your nervous system? Your sense of clarity?

What phrases do they use that seem kind on the surface — but feel off?

How do you tend to respond when someone guilt-trips or gaslights you?

Do you freeze, fawn, over-explain, apologize, retreat, or try to prove your case? Reflect on your protective responses without judgment. They've served a purpose.

How do you tend to respond when someone guilt-trips or gaslights you?

What part of you still feels responsible for their feelings or behavior?

Explore the internalized belief that it's your job to manage everyone's comfort. Where did that belief come from? Is it still serving you — or silently harming you?

What part of you still feels responsible for their feelings or behavior?

How has repeated emotional invalidation affected your self-trust?

Write about how often you second-guess yourself. Have you stopped expressing needs? Apologized for things you didn't do? Gaslit yourself? Let this prompt be a turning point in reclaiming your truth.

How has repeated emotional invalidation affected your self-trust?

What does real support feel like — and how is it different from guilt or control?

Think about someone who genuinely supports you. How do they make space for your feelings? Contrast this with how your in-laws (or others) try to manipulate under the guise of "caring."

What does real support feel like — and how is it different from guilt or control?

What would it mean to stop explaining yourself to people committed to misunderstanding you?

Let yourself feel the relief — and fear — of stepping out of the loop of justification. What would it cost? What would it give you back?

What would it mean to stop explaining yourself to people committed to misunderstanding you?

TRACING THE TRUTH

THE "WHOSE VOICE IS THIS?" MAP

When in-laws gaslight you, their words don't just stay in the room — they often echo in your head long after the conversation ends. Over time, those external voices can start to sound like your own, making you doubt yourself before you even speak. This exercise helps you separate their voice from your voice, so you can begin reclaiming your inner clarity.

Why it helps:
Gaslighting works by infiltration — by planting doubt so deeply that it feels like it originates inside you. Neuroscience shows that labeling thoughts and assigning them back to their source interrupts this confusion. By externalizing the voices, you retrain your nervous system to recognize: this isn't me, it's them.

In the first column, write down gaslighting phrases you've heard from in-laws — word-for-word if you remember them (e.g., "You're imagining things," "You should be grateful," "That never happened.").
In the second column, write your counter-truth. Not the polished, polite version, but the raw truth you felt in the moment (e.g., "I know what I experienced," "I don't need to feel guilty for setting boundaries," "My feelings are valid.").
Once your list is complete, read the two columns aloud. Notice how differently each voice feels in your body. Which voice sounds more like you? Which one carries the weight of control or manipulation?

Circle the statements from your column that feel like anchors — truths you want to come back to when doubt creeps in.

TRACING THE TRUTH

REALITY ANCHORING JOURNAL

| Their Voice in My Head | My True Voice |

TRACING THE TRUTH

SELF VS. OTHER

Gaslighting clouds memory and creates self-doubt. Writing your experiences down gives your nervous system a place to land — a record that can't be erased or argued out of you. This is less about proving anyone wrong and more about reclaiming your trust in yourself.

Why it helps:
The act of recording events in your own words interrupts self-gaslighting. It grounds your reality in black and white and helps you spot patterns of invalidation over time.

Write down a recent situation where you felt dismissed, belittled, or told your perception was "wrong."
Record the facts as you remember them: what was said, what you felt, what your body noticed.
Then, underline one sentence that feels most true to you. That sentence is your anchor.

Revisit this page later — notice if your memory wavered or softened. Let your words remind you: I was there. I know what I experienced.

TRACING THE TRUTH

REALITY ANCHORING JOURNAL

TRACING THE TRUTH

REALITY ANCHORING JOURNAL

ACTION

ENERGY BUDGET

Energy is a limited resource, and most of us spend it like it's endless. By mapping your natural peaks and dips, you begin treating energy the same way you'd treat money — something to spend with intention. Research shows that syncing meaningful tasks with your personal rhythms increases follow-through and reduces burnout. Protecting a rest block is equally vital. Too often, rest is treated as optional, the first thing cut when life gets busy. But rest is where your nervous system resets and your resilience stores refill. By scheduling it like a non-negotiable meeting, you reclaim the truth that your wellbeing is not secondary — it's the foundation.

Map Peaks + Valleys — Track when you feel most alert and when you feel sluggish over 2–3 days. Note the times.

Match Tasks — Place your most meaningful or demanding actions inside your natural energy peaks. Save automatic or lighter tasks for your dips.

Schedule Rest — Block at least one daily rest period (nap, walk, quiet time). Treat it as sacred — no canceling, no apologizing.

ENERGY BUDGET

Energy is a limited resource, and most of us spend it like it's endless. By mapping your natural peaks and dips, you begin treating energy the same way you'd treat money — something to spend with intention. Research shows that syncing meaningful tasks with your personal rhythms increases follow-through and reduces burnout. Protecting a rest block is equally vital. Too often, rest is treated as optional, the first thing cut when life gets busy. But rest is where your nervous system resets and your resilience stores refill. By scheduling it like a non-negotiable meeting, you reclaim the truth that your wellbeing is not secondary — it's the foundation.

Map Peaks + Valleys — Track when you feel most alert and when you feel sluggish over 2–3 days. Note the times.

Match Tasks — Place your most meaningful or demanding actions inside your natural energy peaks. Save automatic or lighter tasks for your dips.

Schedule Rest — Block at least one daily rest period (nap, walk, quiet time). Treat it as sacred — no canceling, no apologizing.

Time	Feeling	Tasks	Notes

SECTION FOUR

Your Nervous System Knows

Sometimes, your body knows long before your mind catches up. Your heart races after a "harmless" comment. Your stomach knots when you see their name on your phone. You leave their house smiling but feel sick for hours afterward. It's easy to dismiss these signs — especially when others tell you you're overreacting or too sensitive. But your body doesn't lie.

Your nervous system is a brilliant, ancient protector. It responds to threats — not just physical danger, but emotional dismissal, manipulation, control, and disconnection. When you're around someone who is emotionally unsafe, your body registers it. And if you've been told to ignore that wisdom for long enough, you may have stopped noticing — or started blaming yourself for reacting.

This section is about remembering that your body has always been telling the truth. We'll explore how to notice those signals, decode them, and begin to trust your internal compass again — no permission needed.

Making Sense Of It
Your Body Knows Before You Do

Polyvagal Theory, developed by Dr. Stephen Porges, helps explain why being around certain people feels like ease and others feel like danger — even if no one raises their voice. At its core, the theory maps how our nervous system shifts between three primary states: ventral vagal (safe and connected), sympathetic (fight or flight), and dorsal vagal (shutdown or freeze). Later trauma research added a fourth pattern: fawn, the reflex to appease and make yourself small.

Around emotionally safe people, your body feels steady, present, maybe even playful. You can disagree without fear of punishment. But when you're in the orbit of a controlling or manipulative in-law, your nervous system doesn't wait for logic — it reacts in real time. A sigh, a dig disguised as a "joke," a reminder that you're an outsider in "their family" — your body registers the threat before your mind has a chance to analyze.

In those moments, you may feel:
- Fight: irritation, clenched jaw, the urge to snap back.
- Flight: overthinking, restless anxiety, the need to leave the room.
- Freeze: emotional numbness, exhaustion, zoning out mid-conversation.
- Fawn: appeasing, laughing at their jokes, smoothing over tension while abandoning your own truth.

These aren't overreactions. They are survival codes written into your body across generations. Anthropology reminds us that humans evolved in tight-knit groups where acceptance was survival.

Making Sense Of It
Your Body Knows Before You Do

What often makes this harder is the cultural layer. In many societies, in-laws hold authority cloaked in tradition — elders are to be respected, harmony must be preserved, family unity comes before individual truth. That conditioning can make it almost impossible to name their behavior as harmful. You may even shame yourself for reacting: Why do I get so tense? Why can't I just brush it off?

Here's the truth: your body is not betraying you. It's protecting you. The tension, the anxiety, the numbness — these are intelligent responses to relational danger. They are signals that something about the dynamic feels unsafe, even if the outside world insists you should smile and be grateful.

When you learn to notice these shifts without judgment, you move out of confusion and into clarity. You start to see: Oh, my stomach knots every time she criticizes me in front of my partner. Or, I dissociate when he makes "jokes" about how I raise the kids. That awareness doesn't just validate your experience — it gives you choices. You may not be able to change your in-law's behavior, but you can learn to trust your body's signals, set firmer boundaries, and stop gaslighting yourself into silence.

Your nervous system isn't overreacting. It's telling the truth your mind has been taught to ignore.

What physical sensations arise when you're around your in-laws — before, during, or after?

Describe how your body responds in detail: Does your chest tighten? Does your jaw clench? Do you feel wired, numb, or heavy? What are the earliest signals that something is off?

What physical sensations arise when you're around your in-laws — before, during, or after?

When do you feel most like you're "walking on eggshells"?

Reflect on specific interactions or environments where your body tenses or your behavior changes to stay safe. How much of your energy goes into managing rather than being?

When do you feel most like you're "walking on eggshells"?

What parts of you try to ignore your body's signals — and why?

Have you ever talked yourself out of leaving a situation your body wanted to escape? Explore what inner narratives override your instincts. ("Don't make a scene," "It's not that bad," "They'll think I'm dramatic.")

What parts of you try to ignore your body's signals — and why?

What does emotional safety feel like in your body?

Shift your attention to times when you felt calm, held, or grounded. What did your breath, posture, and energy feel like? This is your nervous system's baseline — not the chaos.

What does emotional safety feel like in your body?

What sensory cues tend to trigger your nervous system around them?

Is it a tone of voice? A look? A smell or gesture? Begin to identify the triggers that tell your system, "We're not safe here." Awareness leads to choice.

What sensory cues tend to trigger your nervous system around them?

How have you learned to perform calm instead of feeling safe?

Have you smiled while your gut screamed? Sat politely while your muscles screamed to move? Name the difference between compliance and comfort. Your nervous system knows.

How have you learned to perform calm instead of feeling safe?

If your body could speak in words, what would it be trying to tell you about these relationships?

Close your eyes and imagine your body writing you a letter. What would it say? What would it ask of you?

If your body could speak in words, what would it be trying to tell you about these relationships?

TRACING THE TRUTH

MAPPING YOUR BODY'S TRUTH

Your body often tells the story long before your mind can. When you're around in-laws who criticize, dismiss, or manipulate, your nervous system lights up with signals of tension, shutdown, or overdrive. By contrast, when you're with people who feel safe, your body softens and opens. This exercise helps you map those differences side by side, so you can begin trusting your body's wisdom as real evidence — not something to dismiss.

Why it helps:
Gaslighting often makes you question if what you feel is real. But your body doesn't lie. By visually mapping sensations of threat versus safety, you create undeniable evidence that your nervous system's responses are valid. This exercise strengthens self-trust — an essential antidote to the confusion in-law dynamics can create.

Close your eyes. Think of a recent interaction with your in-laws. Scan your body head to toe. On the "WITH THEM" side, color in or label areas of:
    Tension (clenched jaw, tight chest, etc.)
    Numbness (blank mind, heaviness)
    Activation (racing heart, jittery legs)

Now think of a moment when you were with people who made you feel deeply safe. On the "WITHOUT THEM" side, map sensations of:
    Warmth
    Softness
    Groundedness
    Ease

TRACING THE TRUTH

MAPPING YOUR BODY'S TRUTH

With Them 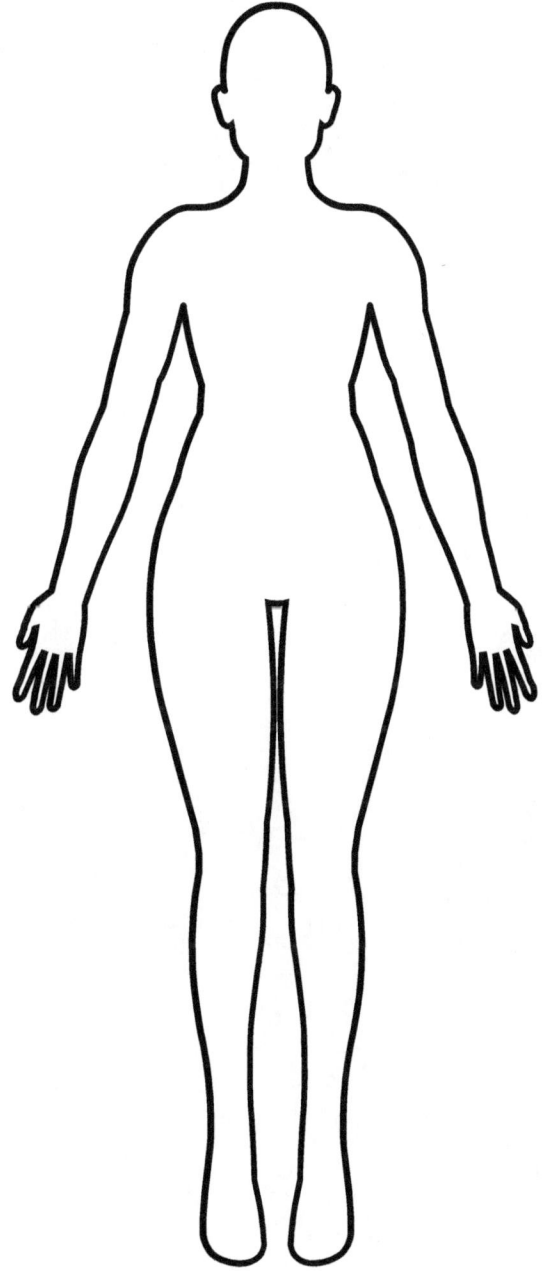 **Without Them**

WINDOW OF TOLERANCE MAP

When you're dysregulated — whether spun up with racing thoughts or shut down and numb — it's almost impossible to think clearly. Mapping your "window of tolerance" gives you a visual reminder of what your nervous system looks and feels like when it's balanced, overstimulated, or under-engaged. Instead of feeling hijacked, you can recognize: "Ah, I'm outside my window right now." That awareness alone widens your choices. It also keeps you from turning regulation into a guessing game; you'll have a personal roadmap of cues and tools that work for you.

Fill in personal cues. For each state, jot what you notice in your body, thoughts, and emotions. (Example: Hyper = clenched jaw, racing mind. Hypo = heavy limbs, flat affect.)

Add regulation tools. Next to Hyper, write 2–3 down-regulating skills (ex: slow breathing, grounding). Next to Hypo, add up-regulating ones (ex: movement, music).

Calm/Present (your window)	Hyper (revved-up)	Hypo (shut-down)
		↓

Regulation Tools

POCKET OF SAFETY

When stress hits, your nervous system automatically searches for threat. Resource installation interrupts that loop by giving your body a felt reminder of safety, strength, or care. Instead of only rehearsing pain, you practice anchoring to something nurturing and stabilizing. This isn't about pretending the hard stuff doesn't exist — it's about teaching your brain and body that safety and support also exist. By pairing the memory with a body cue (like placing your hand on your heart), you create a portable anchor you can return to whenever you feel unsteady. Over time, this strengthens your capacity to self-soothe and widen your window of tolerance.

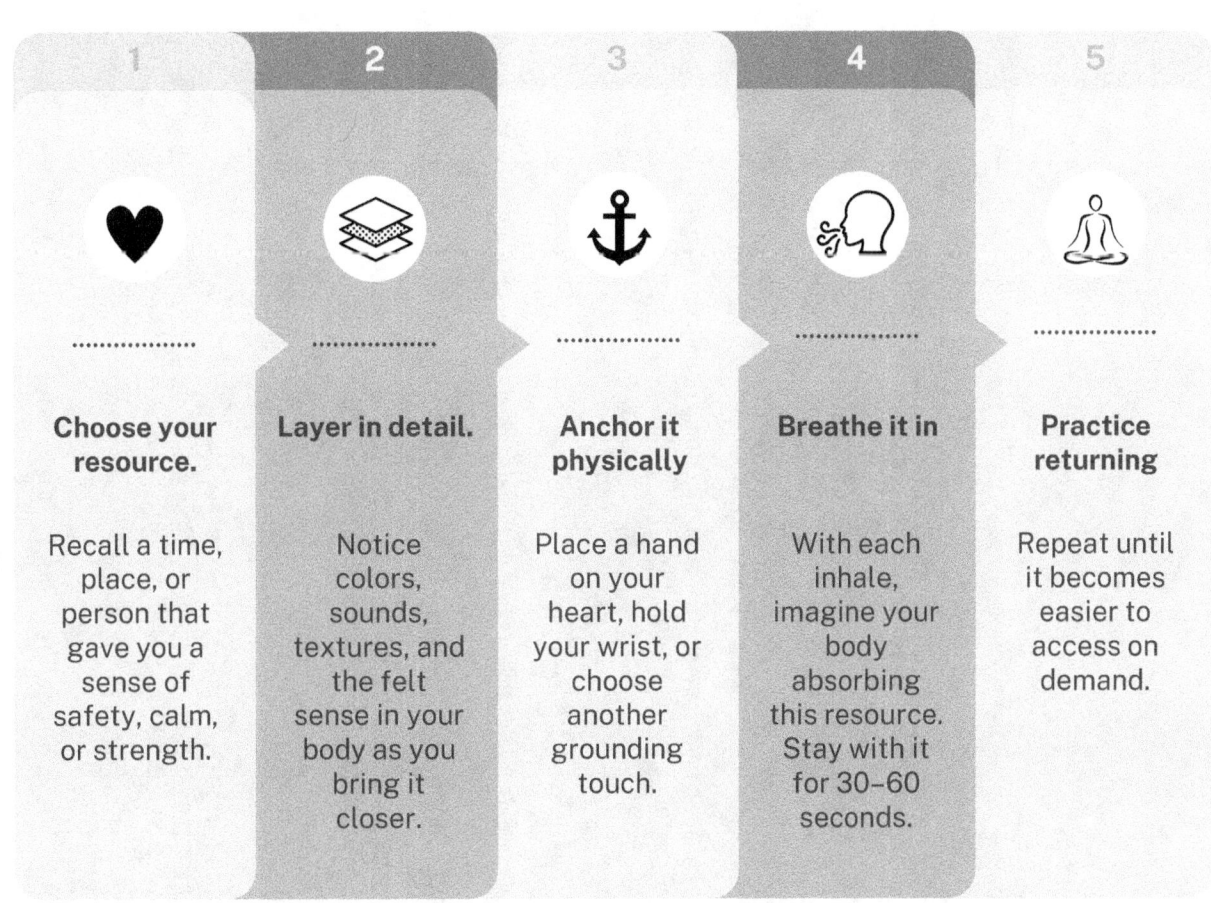

1. Choose your resource. Recall a time, place, or person that gave you a sense of safety, calm, or strength.

2. Layer in detail. Notice colors, sounds, textures, and the felt sense in your body as you bring it closer.

3. Anchor it physically Place a hand on your heart, hold your wrist, or choose another grounding touch.

4. Breathe it in With each inhale, imagine your body absorbing this resource. Stay with it for 30–60 seconds.

5. Practice returning Repeat until it becomes easier to access on demand.

SECTION FIVE

When Your Partner Doesn't See It

One of the deepest betrayals isn't what your in-laws say — it's when your partner doesn't protect you from it. You might feel like you're screaming into a void, trying to explain why their "harmless" behavior leaves you anxious, depleted, or deeply hurt. You may feel like you're the problem, constantly over-explaining, trying not to sound too emotional, all while craving one simple thing: backup.

When the person who's supposed to be your teammate won't — or can't — see the harm being done, it creates a split in your home, your heart, and your sense of reality. You start to question yourself. Is it really that bad? Am I imagining this? Should I just let it go?

This section is about reclaiming your clarity. We'll unpack the trauma of being emotionally unprotected, name the signs of subtle gaslighting, and explore how to reconnect to your truth — even if no one else validates it yet.

Making Sense Of It
When Your Partner Doesn't See It

Few things cut deeper than realizing the person who should be your safe harbor doesn't recognize the storm you're weathering. When your partner refuses to acknowledge harmful in-law behavior, you're placed in what trauma psychologists call a double bind: no matter what you do, you lose. If you speak up, you risk being labeled "too sensitive," "dramatic," or "ungrateful." If you stay quiet, you betray yourself and allow the harm to continue unchecked. Either path costs you safety.

Attachment theory tells us that emotional safety inside a partnership is the foundation of secure bonding. Ideally, when your nervous system is rattled — whether by a cruel comment, a humiliating "joke," or constant undermining from your in-laws — your partner should help regulate the rupture. But when your pain is minimized, dismissed, or denied by the one person you rely on most, your attachment system doesn't just wobble; it fractures. What should have been co-regulation becomes aloneness, which the nervous system reads as abandonment.

This abandonment isn't only emotional. Anthropologically, marriage has long meant joining a larger kinship system. In many cultures, loyalty to the extended family is prized, sometimes even above loyalty to the spouse. When your partner unconsciously aligns with their family over you, it taps into centuries-old patterns of kinship politics: insiders are protected, outsiders must earn their place. In that light, your experience isn't simply interpersonal tension — it's a clash between individual needs and collective loyalty, which explains why it feels so destabilizing.

Making Sense Of It
When Your Partner Doesn't See It

Over time, this dynamic breeds internalized gaslighting. You begin questioning yourself: Maybe I am exaggerating. Maybe it wasn't that bad. Maybe if I were stronger, I wouldn't feel this way. This erosion of self-trust is trauma in slow motion. It's not "family drama." It's relational abandonment disguised as keeping the peace. Being unseen, especially when the harm is subtle or socially sanctioned, creates a wound as real as any betrayal.

Your pain in these moments is not weakness. It's your body and psyche registering the truth: that partnership without recognition of harm is not safety, it's isolation. Healing begins not with forcing your partner to change, but with reclaiming your own perception as valid, your emotional signals as trustworthy, and your right to be protected as non-negotiable.

What makes this even more painful is the invisibility of it. If your in-laws shouted at you or openly insulted you, the harm would be undeniable. But because it often comes wrapped in politeness, backhanded compliments, or "tradition," you're left holding the weight of something no one else names. And when your partner refuses to witness it, you're forced into the loneliest role of all: both victim and silent witness to your own pain. That's why this isn't a matter of being "thin-skinned." It's the disorienting reality of enduring harm while being told it doesn't exist — a form of abandonment that leaves scars not just on your relationship, but on your sense of self.

When have you most needed your partner to protect or stand up for you — and what happened instead?

Revisit specific memories, even small ones. What did you hope they would say or do? What did you feel in the silence or dismissal?

When have you most needed your partner to protect or stand up for you — and what happened instead?

How does your partner's response make you doubt yourself?

List the thoughts that rise when they downplay your experience. Are there phrases you hear in your own head now that sound like their voice?

How does your partner's response make you doubt yourself?

What would it feel like to be fully emotionally backed by your partner?

Imagine that version of them for a moment — not to escape, but to get clear on what safety actually looks like. What changes in your body, voice, confidence?

What would it feel like to be fully emotionally backed by your partner?

What fears might your partner have that prevent them from validating you?

Step into compassion — not to excuse the harm, but to better understand what keeps them "neutral." Are they afraid of conflict? Of disappointing their family? Of being "caught in the middle"?

What fears might your partner have that prevent them from validating you?

What part of you has stayed silent to avoid rocking the boat — and what has it cost you?

Trace the emotional labor you've taken on. Who have you been protecting — and who's been protecting you?

What part of you has stayed silent to avoid rocking the boat — and what has it cost you?

What does it mean to trust your reality, even when others don't?

Explore what it would take to anchor in your own emotional truth — even when you feel alone in it. What would you stop explaining, justifying, or shrinking?

What does it mean to trust your reality, even when others don't?

What boundary — internal or external — wants to be named or honored now?

This might not be something you act on yet. Just name it. What truth wants out? What clarity wants space?

What boundary — internal or external — wants to be named or honored now?

TRACING THE TRUTH

THE UNHEARD VOICE

Silence in the face of harm is its own wound. Writing out your story gives voice to the part of you that was left alone in the room. This is not about blaming, but about reclaiming your truth and honoring what you needed but didn't receive.

Why it helps:
Narrative rewriting allows your nervous system to process unfinished moments of abandonment. By naming what you needed, you release the shame of "expecting too much" and affirm that your longing for safety was valid.

Recall a specific moment when your in-laws hurt you and your partner failed to respond.
Write the story in two short parts:
What Happened: Describe the incident factually. Include what was said, how your partner reacted (or didn't), and what you felt in your body.
What I Needed: Write the response you longed for — the words, the protection, the validation. Be as specific and unfiltered as you can.
End with this line: "I deserved to be protected, and my pain deserved to be seen." Write it as many times as you need until it feels real in your body.

TRACING THE TRUTH

THE UNHEARD VOICE

TRACING THE TRUTH

THE UNHEARD VOICE

TRACING THE TRUTH

THE UNHEARD VOICE

TRACING THE TRUTH

THE LOYALTY VENN DIAGRAM

When your partner minimizes or ignores in-law harm, it can feel like they've chosen sides. But often the reality is more complicated — they may feel torn between loyalty to you and loyalty to their family of origin. This exercise helps you see where loyalties overlap, where they're divided, and where you've been left standing alone.

Why it helps:
Gaslighting thrives in ambiguity. Putting experiences into clear categories helps you see the pattern — not as drama, but as evidence. This clarity helps you stop doubting your own experience.

In the "Me" circle, write examples of times your partner has clearly shown up for you, validated your reality, or set a boundary with their family in your defense.
In the "Family" circle, list times they've taken their family's side, dismissed your experience, or prioritized family peace over your well-being.
In the overlap, write situations where their actions tried to keep both sides happy but left you feeling unseen or unprotected.

Step back and ask: Does the overlap feel like true balance, or like avoidance at my expense? Let the diagram clarify what your body already knows.

TRACING THE TRUTH

THE LOYALTY VENN DIAGRAM

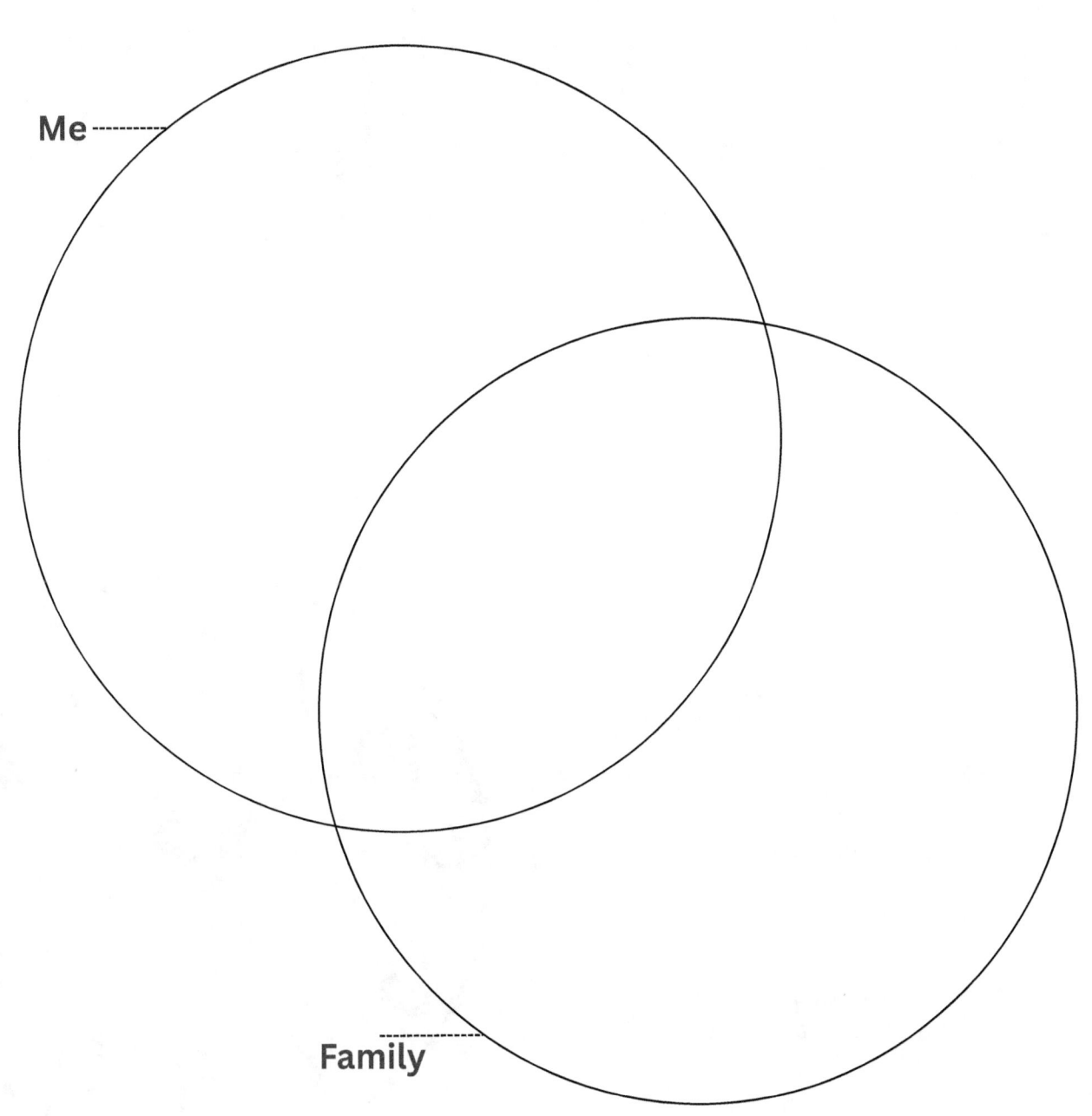

WORRY WINDOW

Worries often hijack your mind, showing up at every unexpected moment. By giving them a dedicated "time slot," you reclaim control instead of letting them run your day. This practice teaches your nervous system that there's a safe space and a safe time to process, so you're not constantly reacting to every intrusive thought. During the window, you can gently evaluate what's actionable versus what you need to let go, building clarity and self-trust. Outside the window, a simple cue like "not now—later" helps you return to the present without guilt or shame. Over time, this simple structure reduces the intensity and frequency of anxious loops.

Park your worries: Write them down as they arise.

....

....

....

....

Set a 15-minute window: Choose a consistent time each day for processing.

....

Outside the window: Use a cue phrase like "not now—later" to return to your day.

Inside the window: Review the list. Solve what's actionable, accept what isn't, and release judgment.

Close the window: End with a grounding or soothing activity to signal completion.

GENTLE BREATH FOCUS

When anxiety spikes, the mind and body race together — thoughts accelerate, heart rate climbs, muscles tighten. Counting your breath gives both something steady to follow. By pairing inhale and exhale with numbers, you create a gentle anchor that slows the nervous system, refocuses attention, and interrupts spiraling thoughts. This isn't about perfection or achieving ten — it's about returning to the rhythm whenever distraction occurs. Even a few minutes daily strengthens your capacity to notice tension, settle your body, and move through anxious moments with less overwhelm.

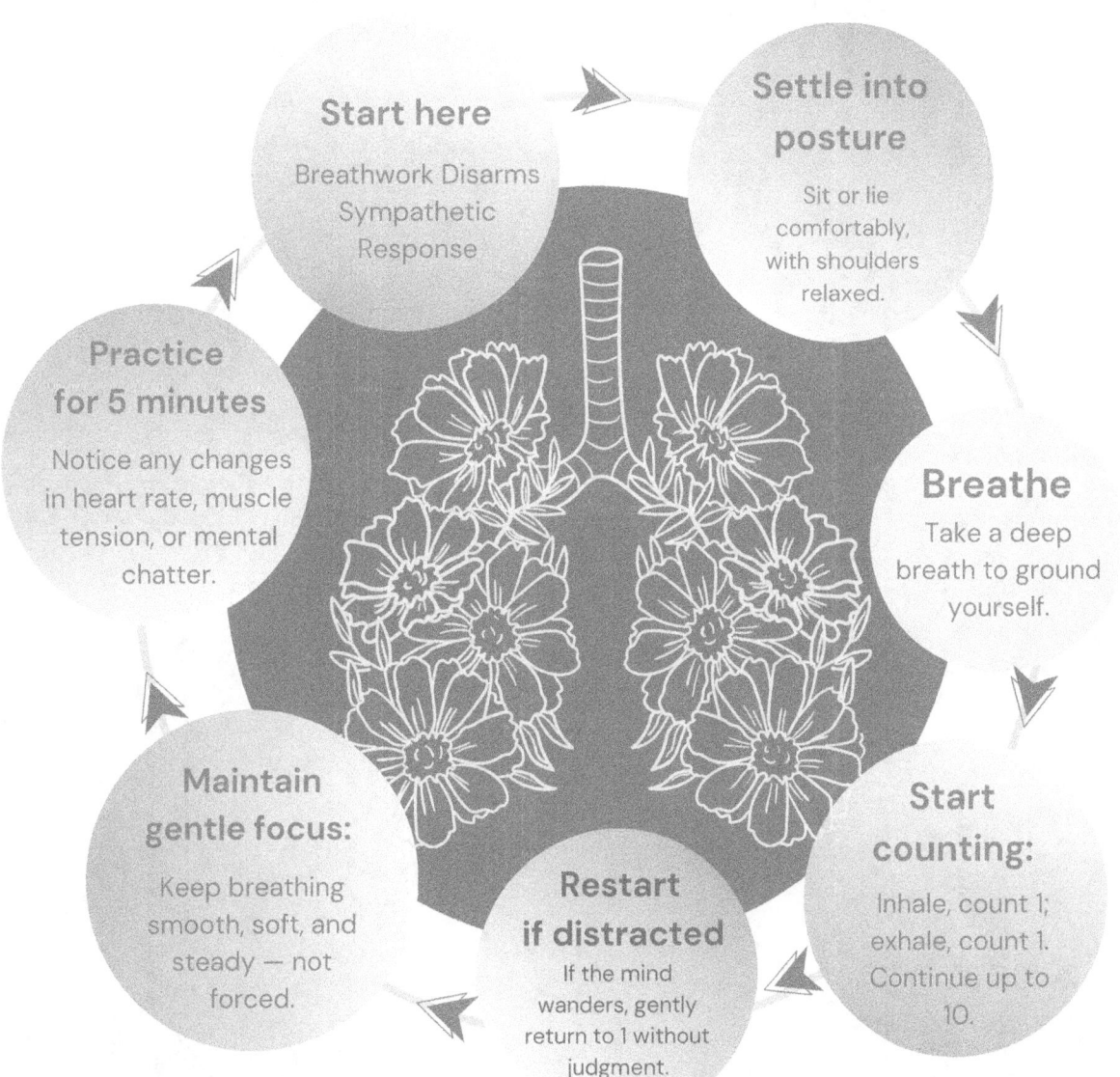

Start here
Breathwork Disarms Sympathetic Response

Settle into posture
Sit or lie comfortably, with shoulders relaxed.

Breathe
Take a deep breath to ground yourself.

Start counting:
Inhale, count 1; exhale, count 1. Continue up to 10.

Restart if distracted
If the mind wanders, gently return to 1 without judgment.

Maintain gentle focus:
Keep breathing smooth, soft, and steady — not forced.

Practice for 5 minutes
Notice any changes in heart rate, muscle tension, or mental chatter.

SECTION SIX

Emotional Puppeteering – Guilt Trips, Gifts with Strings, and Control Disguised as Care

Sometimes control doesn't look like yelling or insults. It shows up wrapped in a casserole. It sounds like "I was just trying to help." It hides behind favors you didn't ask for, holidays you feel forced to attend, or gifts that come with invisible strings. You're told it's love, but it feels like pressure — and when you try to say no, you're hit with guilt, cold shoulders, or family whispers that paint you as ungrateful.

This isn't petty. This is emotional manipulation — and it's real. Being pulled by guilt, obligation, or fear of fallout is not the same as choosing from love.

In this section, we'll name the most common manipulation tactics toxic in-laws use, help you identify how they hook into your nervous system, and begin untangling your identity from their expectations. This is where you take your power back — not by becoming cruel, but by becoming clear.

Making Sense Of It
Covert Control and the Trauma of "Nice"

Emotional manipulation within in-law relationships is one of the most subtle yet devastating forces in family life. Unlike overt conflict — raised voices, direct insults, or clear betrayals — this form of control often arrives coated in sugar, wrapped in the language of love, or disguised as tradition and "family values." It's hard to name, even harder to confront, because on the surface it doesn't look like cruelty. It looks like care. And yet, beneath the surface, it erodes your autonomy, reshapes your nervous system responses, and keeps you bound in a cycle of guilt, fear, and compliance.

Here's how it tends to appear:
- Guilt-tripping: "After everything we've done for you..."
- Withholding: "Well, if you can't make it, I guess we just won't come at all."
- Martyrdom: "I was only trying to help. I don't know why I always get painted as the bad one."
- Enmeshment: "If you truly loved this family, you wouldn't need so much space."

Individually, these statements may seem small. Collectively, they create a pattern where your emotions, choices, and boundaries are consistently questioned — not with outright aggression, but with carefully crafted pressure. The end result? You learn that peace comes only when you silence yourself.

Making Sense Of It
Covert Control and the Trauma of "Nice"

From an anthropological perspective, this behavior often grows out of generational family systems. In many cultures, family loyalty is equated with survival. The unspoken rule is: you don't turn away from blood. For a parent, losing influence over their adult child — or worse, having that child shift allegiance to a spouse — can feel like abandonment. In-laws may then double down with covert tactics, not because they consciously want to harm, but because it restores their sense of control within the "tribe." It's the old survival code playing out in modern kitchens and living rooms.

But what feels like loyalty to them often translates into bondage for you. The human nervous system, designed to keep us safe, interprets these moments of covert coercion as relational danger. Maybe you notice your jaw clench when they walk in the door, or your chest tighten when you see their name on your phone. This isn't you being "too sensitive." It's your body recognizing the unspoken threat: If you resist, you'll pay.

This is where the fawn response emerges. Unlike fight, flight, or freeze, fawning is about appeasement — smiling while you're shrinking, nodding while you're silently screaming no. For many, fawning begins as a child's survival tactic in unpredictable households. But when in-laws weaponize guilt, martyrdom, or enmeshment, it reactivates that old strategy. You find yourself playing small, keeping the peace, protecting your partner from tension — all while abandoning your own truth.

Making Sense Of It
Covert Control and the Trauma of "Nice"

The long-term effect is what psychologists call internalized shame. You begin to question whether you're selfish for setting limits, whether you're ungrateful for wanting independence, whether your anger is even legitimate. You may even start gaslighting yourself, telling your own body to "calm down" when it's actually sounding the alarm. That's how deep this conditioning runs.

And here's the hardest part: society often colludes with the manipulation. How many times have you heard, "That's just how she is, you've got to accept it," or "Family is everything, don't make waves"? These cultural messages reinforce the idea that your discomfort is less important than the family image. But emotional coercion is not love. It's control disguised as care. Real love does not need you to shrink to fit. Real safety does not require your silence. Real family allows space for difference without weaponizing loyalty.

The truth is, recognizing manipulation is not about villainizing your in-laws. It's about reclaiming your own clarity and refusing to keep trading self-abandonment for temporary peace. You don't owe anyone your silence at the cost of your soul.

What "gifts" have come with invisible strings or expectations attached?

Describe a time you received something — a favor, money, visit, support — and later felt controlled or indebted. What did you feel but not say?

What "gifts" have come with invisible strings or expectations attached?

How does guilt show up when you try to make a decision they won't like?

Does it sound like a voice in your head? A sinking feeling in your stomach? Whose approval are you afraid of losing?

How does guilt show up when you try to make a decision they won't like?

When have you felt like saying "no" but said "yes" to avoid fallout?

Trace the moment: What did you fear would happen if you set a boundary? What would you need in place (internal or external) to say "no" next time?

When have you felt like saying "no" but said "yes" to avoid fallout?

What part of you still feels responsible for their feelings?

Where did that role begin? Were you taught that kindness means compliance? That keeping the peace is your job?

What part of you still feels responsible for their feelings?

What's the difference between love and obligation, in your body?

Think of a moment when you gave freely and joyfully. Now contrast it with one where you acted from guilt. What changed in your breath, shoulders, energy?

What's the difference between love and obligation, in your body?

What would your choices look like if you were free from guilt?

Imagine a version of yourself that doesn't second-guess, apologize, or over-explain. What decisions would you make differently?

What would your choices look like if you were free from guilt?

TRACING THE TRUTH

THE FAMILY MIRROR

Manipulation thrives in systems where silence is expected. This exercise helps you place manipulative tactics in the wider family culture — so you can see that the pressure didn't begin with you, and it doesn't belong to you.

Why it helps:
By situating manipulation within generational or cultural patterns, you stop personalizing it. This perspective shift helps release the "it must be me" narrative and makes space for healthier boundaries.

Inside the mirror, write down the manipulative phrases or behaviors you've experienced (guilt, withholding, martyrdom, etc.).
Outside the mirror, around the frame, write where you think these behaviors come from: cultural expectations, gender roles, religious obligations, generational trauma, family loyalty, fear of losing control, etc.

Reflect in writing: What changes in me when I see this behavior as part of a bigger system, rather than a personal flaw?

TRACING THE TRUTH

THE FAMILY MIRROR

TRACING THE TRUTH

THE FAMILY MIRROR

Reflection:

TRACING THE TRUTH

THE PLAYBACK TEST

Manipulation is slippery because it often sounds "reasonable" in the moment. This exercise lets you step outside the interaction and hear it from another perspective.

Why it helps:
By replaying the exchange as though you were an observer, you unhook from shame and see the tactic for what it is — not love, not care, but control.

Write out a short dialogue from a recent manipulative moment with your in-law. Try to keep their words verbatim.
On the next line, write your response. Be honest — include what you actually said (or didn't say).
Now, re-read the script as if you're watching two characters in a movie.
Ask yourself:
Would I call this "caring" if I overheard strangers speaking this way?
How does the "caring" language mask control?
What do I feel in my body when I read it back?
End by writing: "What I see now, that I couldn't see then, is _____."

TRACING THE TRUTH

THE PLAYBACK TEST

TRACING THE TRUTH

THE PLAYBACK TEST

TRACING THE TRUTH

THE PLAYBACK TEST

ACTION

PROGRESSIVE MUSCLE RELAXATION

When stress lingers, tension builds in muscles without us noticing, keeping the nervous system on high alert. PMR gently signals to your body that it's safe to let go. By intentionally tensing and then releasing each muscle group, you highlight the difference between tension and relaxation, training your body to notice and release stress. This practice doesn't just relax the muscles—it communicates to your nervous system that it can downshift, making calm feel real and accessible.

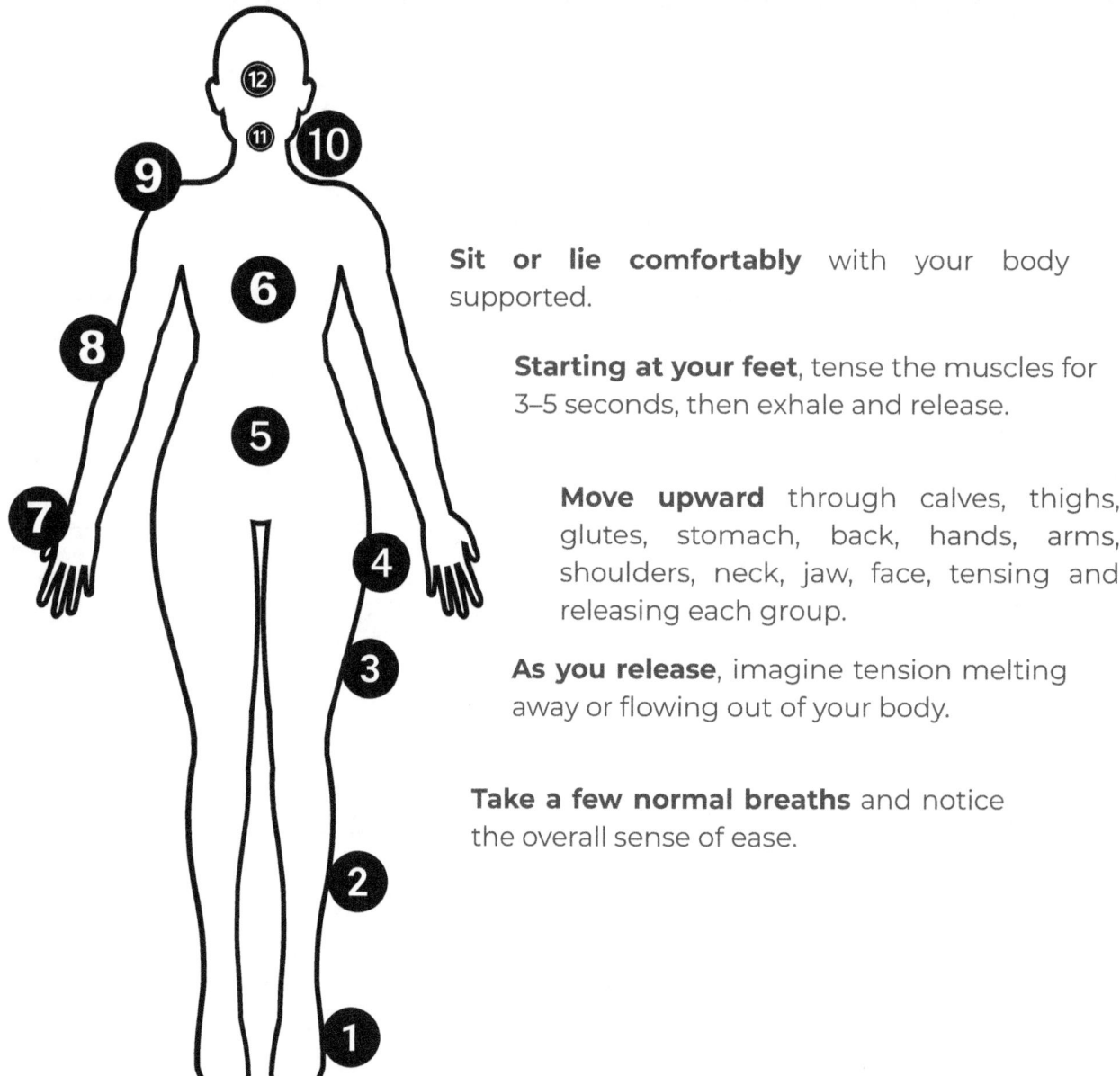

Sit or lie comfortably with your body supported.

Starting at your feet, tense the muscles for 3–5 seconds, then exhale and release.

Move upward through calves, thighs, glutes, stomach, back, hands, arms, shoulders, neck, jaw, face, tensing and releasing each group.

As you release, imagine tension melting away or flowing out of your body.

Take a few normal breaths and notice the overall sense of ease.

ACTION

THE VOO RESET

Our vagus nerve connects the brain and body, regulating stress and calm. Gentle vocalization, like a long "voo" on the exhale, stimulates this pathway, sending a signal that it's safe to downshift arousal. The vibration through your chest and throat also grounds your attention in your body, giving your nervous system tangible proof that it can relax. Just a few rounds can reduce tension, slow your heart rate, and invite a sense of ease.

Sit or stand comfortably with shoulders relaxed.

Inhale slowly through your nose.

Exhale while vocalizing a long, gentle "voo," letting your chest and throat vibrate.

Repeat for 3 rounds, noticing the sensations and any shift in tension.

Place a hand on your chest to feel the vibration more clearly.

SECTION SEVEN

When Kids Are Involved – Protecting Your Children from Toxic Dynamics Without Losing Yourself

When you have kids, everything gets more complicated. What you might have tolerated before — the snide remarks, boundary crossings, manipulations — suddenly feels intolerable when little eyes are watching. You're not just managing your own nervous system anymore. You're protecting theirs.

But trying to buffer your children from toxic in-laws while also preserving your sanity, your relationship, and your sense of self? It can feel like an emotional high-wire act with no net.

This section is for the parents caught in the middle — trying to protect without poisoning, trying to be honest without causing harm, trying to parent from truth while navigating pressure to play nice. We'll explore what it means to be a cycle-breaker, how to model emotional safety for your kids even when extended family isn't safe, and how to choose your child's wellbeing and your own — even when others won't understand.

Making Sense Of It
Attachment, Legacy Trauma, and Emotional Modeling

One of the hardest things about manipulative in-laws is how subtle it often looks from the outside. They're not screaming or throwing things. Instead, it comes wrapped in politeness, family loyalty, or even what sounds like care. You hear things like: "After all we've done for you…" or "I was only trying to help — sorry you're so sensitive." These comments may sound small, but they cut deep. They're designed to make you second-guess yourself, to turn the spotlight away from their behavior and onto your reaction. And slowly, you start asking: Am I the problem? Am I being selfish? Am I imagining this?

The reason this hits so hard isn't because you're weak — it's because most of us are wired to crave belonging. Families, in every culture, have always used guilt and obligation to keep everyone in line. Being "good" often means respecting elders, keeping harmony, and not rocking the boat. So when in-laws use guilt or martyrdom ("We just won't come, then"), they aren't only tugging on your emotions. They're tugging on old survival instincts — the ones that say, "If I'm not accepted, I won't be safe." Of course it feels overwhelming. Of course it feels easier to just give in.

The problem is, that survival strategy comes at a cost. Your body feels the truth before your mind does — the jaw that tightens when they criticize you, the stomach that flips when you know a phone call is coming, the heaviness that settles after yet another boundary gets crossed.

Making Sense Of It
Attachment, Legacy Trauma, and Emotional Modeling

Deep down, your nervous system knows something isn't right. But your mind argues with itself: Maybe they didn't mean it. Maybe I'm too harsh. Maybe it's just family dynamics. That constant tug-of-war is exhausting. It leaves you disconnected from your own instincts, like you can't quite trust yourself anymore.

This is why so many people slide into what's called the "fawn response" — pleasing, appeasing, smiling, smoothing things over. Not because they're weak, but because in the moment, it feels safer than being labeled difficult or ungrateful. It's a way of protecting yourself. But over time, fawning slowly erases your voice. You find yourself going along with things you never agreed to, shrinking parts of yourself just to avoid the fallout, or feeling like you're living someone else's version of your life.

Here's the truth you may need to hear: love never requires you to disappear. Respect doesn't mean self-erasure. And if the price of "keeping the peace" is abandoning your own peace of mind, that's not family loyalty — that's control. Naming it for what it is doesn't make you ungrateful or dramatic. It makes you free.

What have your kids witnessed that made you uncomfortable — and why?

Think back to interactions between your in-laws and your children. What did your body feel? What did you wish you could have said or done in the moment?

What have your kids witnessed that made you uncomfortable — and why?

When do you feel pressure to "keep the peace" for the kids' sake?

Who taught you that peace comes from silence? What might true peace look like — not just absence of conflict, but presence of emotional honesty?

When do you feel pressure to "keep the peace" for the kids' sake?

How did your own childhood experiences shape your boundaries now?

Were you protected from toxic family behavior, or taught to normalize it? What did you wish someone had done for you?

How did your own childhood experiences shape your boundaries now?

What legacy are you choosing to interrupt?

Name one harmful belief, pattern, or dynamic from your family or your in-laws that you refuse to pass on. How does that make you feel — empowered, afraid, conflicted?

What legacy are you choosing to interrupt?

How can you talk to your children about difficult family members in age-appropriate ways?

What truths can you offer that neither shame nor scapegoat, but teach discernment and emotional safety?

How can you talk to your children about difficult family members in age-appropriate ways?

What part of you still feels afraid to disappoint your in-laws — even for your child's sake?

Where does that fear live in your body? What would that part need to feel safer speaking up?

What part of you still feels afraid to disappoint your in-laws — even for your child's sake?

TRACING THE TRUTH

TRANSLATION TABLE — FROM MANIPULATION TO TRUTH

Manipulative comments are powerful because they sound almost reasonable. This exercise helps you strip away the false layer and name what's really being said.

Why it helps:
When you translate manipulative language into its true meaning, you stop carrying the shame of their words. Instead, you see the tactic clearly and reclaim your clarity.

On the left, write down three to five real phrases you've heard from your in-laws. For example:
"We were just trying to help."
"I guess we just won't come then."
"After all we've done for you…"
In the right column, write the translation. Examples:
"We want control over how you live your life."
"If you don't comply, we'll punish you with withdrawal."
"We expect endless gratitude and obedience."

Step back and read the right-hand column out loud. Notice how different it feels when the mask comes off.

TRACING THE TRUTH

TRANSLATION TABLE — FROM MANIPULATION TO TRUTH

WHAT THEY SAID   WHAT IT REALLY MEANS

TRACING THE TRUTH

GIVING YOUR VOICE BACK

Manipulation works by shrinking your voice. This exercise is about giving it back — even if only on the page, at first.

Why it helps:
Writing the words you couldn't say out loud lets your nervous system practice reclaiming power in a safe way. It helps untangle your truth from the web of shame.

Think of one manipulative moment that still lingers in your body.
On one side of the page, write down exactly what they said.
On the next page, write: "What I wish I could have said…" and let yourself respond freely. Don't worry about sounding polite, reasonable, or "family appropriate." This is your uncensored truth.

Read your response back slowly. Notice what shifts inside you when your voice finally has space to exist.
End the page with this affirmation: "My truth matters, even when others refuse to hear it."

TRACING THE TRUTH

GIVING YOUR VOICE BACK

TRACING THE TRUTH

GIVING YOUR VOICE BACK

ACTION

LEAVES ON A STREAM

We often get stuck in our thoughts, treating them as commands or facts, which fuels stress and emotional overwhelm. Defusion teaches you to step back and see thoughts as just thoughts—mental events that come and go. By visualizing them on leaves drifting down a stream, you give your mind space to notice them without reacting. This practice reduces the pull of negative thinking, strengthens present-moment awareness, and improves emotional flexibility.

Sit quietly and settle. Take a few slow breaths, noticing your body and surroundings.

Visualize the stream. Picture a gentle stream flowing in front of you.

Place thoughts on leaves. Each time a thought appears, imagine putting it on a leaf floating by.

Label hooked moments. If you notice you're caught up in a thought, gently label it "thinking" and return it to the stream.

Continue for 5–10 minutes. Keep observing without judgment, letting each thought drift away.

ACTION

MOMENT-TO-MOMENT AWARENESS

Our minds are constantly busy—hearing, thinking, planning, feeling—and it's easy to get swept away in the stream of thoughts and sensations. This practice helps you step back and notice what's happening in the present without getting stuck. By softly labeling each experience, you create a gentle separation between yourself and the flood of mental activity. Even a short daily practice trains your attention, lowers emotional reactivity, and strengthens the ability to return to calm focus when life gets overwhelming.

Set a timer for 5 minutes so you can fully commit without checking the clock.

Sit comfortably and close your eyes if you like.

Notice experiences as they arise. Softly label them as: "hearing... thinking... planning... feeling..."

Return to your breath. After labeling, bring your attention back to your natural breathing.

Repeat gently. Whenever your mind wanders, notice it, label it, and return to the breath without judgment.

SECTION EIGHT

The Partner Problem – When They Don't See It, Don't Believe You, or Don't Want to Rock the Boat

It's one thing to deal with a toxic in-law. It's another thing entirely when the person you love — the one who should have your back — stays silent, stays neutral, or even sides with the dysfunction.

This section is for the heartbreak of feeling alone in your own relationship. For the confusion of second-guessing what you felt, what you saw, what you know was wrong — because your partner won't name it with you. Maybe they're conflict-avoidant, frozen by guilt, or still emotionally enmeshed. Maybe they've never had to look at their family through the lens you now carry: trauma, boundaries, truth.

Whatever the reason, the result is often the same: you're hurt, you're angry, and you're stuck between being silent and being "too much." This section helps you reclaim your clarity, rebuild trust, and learn how to speak your truth — even when the person closest to you doesn't want to hear it.

Making Sense Of It
Attachment Styles, Fawn Responses, and Loyalty Binds

When your partner defends or minimizes a toxic parent, it doesn't always mean they don't love you. More often, it means they've been living inside a system that trained them to protect their parent at all costs. What you're running into isn't always betrayal — it's often an unexamined trauma bond.

For many adult children of toxic parents, survival meant loyalty. They were taught, directly or indirectly, that questioning authority was dangerous, that love had to be earned, and that peace in the household depended on their ability to shrink, appease, or smooth things over. Maybe they were punished for speaking up. Maybe their needs were ignored until they stopped naming them. Maybe "good kids" were praised for obedience while "difficult" ones were shamed. These lessons sink deep into the body. Long before your partner met you, their nervous system was already wired to choose harmony with their parent over honesty with themselves.

This is what's known as a loyalty bind — a subconscious belief that protecting the image of the parent is more important than protecting the truth of the relationship. In many families, this is reinforced through cultural or generational values: "family comes first," "blood is thicker than water," or "you only get one mother." On the surface, these sayings look like wisdom. But underneath, they act like handcuffs. They make defending the parent seem virtuous, even when it causes harm to everyone else.

Making Sense Of It
Attachment Styles, Fawn Responses, and Loyalty Binds

Your partner may not even realize they're doing this. To them, minimizing your pain may feel like the only way to keep the family system intact. They might say, "That's just how she is," or "You're overthinking it," not because they don't see your hurt, but because admitting it would force them to confront a lifetime of painful truths. Denial is a survival mechanism too. It keeps them connected to the parent they still, on some level, depend on — even if that parent is manipulative or controlling.

But here's the reality: understanding your partner's bind doesn't erase the impact on you. Their refusal to confront the truth still leaves you carrying the weight. That's why healing starts with clarity inside yourself. You don't need their permission to call what happened by its real name. You don't need them to agree before you set boundaries that protect you. What you do need is support, validation, and practices that anchor you back to your own sense of reality — especially when family loyalty scripts try to pull you under. And here's something worth holding onto: loyalty that demands silence isn't love. It's fear in disguise. Real love doesn't ask you to vanish so someone else's image can stay polished. Real love allows the truth to breathe — even when it's uncomfortable.

What have you tried to express to your partner — and how was it received?

Get specific about one moment that left you feeling dismissed, gaslit, or emotionally abandoned. What did your body feel in that moment?

What have you tried to express to your partner — and how was it received?

How does your partner's relationship with their parent mirror patterns you've seen before?

Are they acting like a peacekeeper? A scared child? A guilt-trapped adult? What do you think they're really afraid of?

How does your partner's relationship with their parent mirror patterns you've seen before?

When do you feel pressure to "let it go" for the sake of your relationship?

What does letting go actually mean — emotional numbness, silence, pretending? What does it cost you?

When do you feel pressure to "let it go" for the sake of your relationship?

What would feeling seen and backed up by your partner look and sound like?

Describe a moment you've longed for — where they defended you, validated your pain, or chose your wellbeing out loud.

What would feeling seen and backed up by your partner look and sound like?

What part of you still doubts your right to make this a problem?

Explore the internalized voices that say: "Don't be dramatic," "They didn't mean it," "You're making things worse." Whose voice is that, really?

What part of you still doubts your right to make this a problem?

What happens in your body when your partner sides with their parent over you — even subtly?

Where does it live? What does it remind you of? What would that part of you need to feel safe again?

What happens in your body when your partner sides with their parent over you — even subtly?

TRACING THE TRUTH

THE IMPACT WEB

Loyalty binds ripple far beyond a single moment. This exercise helps you see the real impact of a partner's defense of their parent — without blaming them.

Why it helps:
Visualizing the ripples separates your partner's past trauma from the ongoing effects on you. It highlights where you can reclaim control and start prioritizing your well-being.

Draw a small circle in the center of your page and write: "Defending the Parent / Minimizing My Pain."
From that circle, draw lines outward like a web. At the end of each line, write a ripple effect on your life — e.g., anxiety, tension with your partner, sleepless nights, self-doubt, missed opportunities to speak your truth.
Add another layer: what parts of you are affected? Energy, confidence, voice, peace of mind, relationships with friends or kids.

Reflect in writing: "Which of these ripples do I have the power to reduce or redirect?"

TRACING THE TRUTH

THE IMPACT WEB

TRACING THE TRUTH

THE IMPACT WEB

Reflection:

TRACING THE TRUTH

THE "IF I HAD PERMISSION" LETTER

Sometimes we wait for permission to feel, name, or protect our own truth. This exercise bypasses that wait.

Why it helps:
Writing as if permission is already granted gives your nervous system a rehearsal space. It strengthens internal clarity and reduces the power of loyalty binds, so you can respond consciously instead of reacting out of old patterns.

Start by writing: "If I had full permission to speak my truth and protect myself…"
Complete the sentence with whatever comes naturally: feelings you've withheld, boundaries you want to set, or things you wish you could have said to your partner or in-laws.
Continue for 1–2 pages, letting yourself write freely. Don't worry about politeness or outcomes — this is for your clarity, not theirs.

End with a closing affirmation: "I don't need permission to honor my experience. I am allowed to be safe and seen."

TRACING THE TRUTH

THE "IF I HAD PERMISSION" LETTER

TRACING THE TRUTH

THE "IF I HAD PERMISSION" LETTER

TRACING THE TRUTH

THE "IF I HAD PERMISSION" LETTER

ACTION

KIND INTENTION SETTING

Intentions are like a quiet compass. They don't pressure you or set you up to "succeed" or "fail." They just give you something gentle to return to when the day gets noisy. Starting your morning with one small sentence helps you set the tone: maybe you want to be steadier, softer, braver. Ending the day with another sentence helps you notice where you actually showed up, without the self-punishment. It's less about performance and more about self-trust — proof that you can guide yourself kindly, one day at a time.

Morning: Write one line — "Today, I will show up with ___." (e.g., patience, presence, steadiness).

_____

Carry it lightly: Let it sit in the back of your mind; check in when you feel pulled off course.

Evening: Write one line — "Today, I showed up with ___." Be honest, but kind.

_____

Close the loop: Let the day go. Tomorrow is fresh.

ACTION

SOFTENING FROM THE OUTSIDE IN

Your body posture is like a shortcut to your nervous system. When your fists are clenched and your face is tight, your body signals danger and your mind follows suit. But when you open your hands and soften your expression, you flip that message: I don't have to fight right now. This simple shift can bring down stress levels in real time, reminding you that you have choices in how you respond.

1 Sit
Comfortably with both feet grounded.

2 Place your hands
palms facing up, on your thighs. Let them rest as if they have nothing to hold. Let your eyes relax.

3 Soften your jaw
relax your eyebrows, drop your tongue from the roof of your mouth, and drop your shoulders.

4 Take 2–3 slow breaths
Notice how your body feels when it isn't bracing for impact.

SECTION NINE

When You Have Kids – Protecting Their Peace Without Inheriting the Dysfunction

Parenting is already a vulnerable, high-stakes job. But parenting while navigating toxic in-laws? That's a minefield. You're not just managing behavior — you're managing legacy. Trying to give your kids the love, boundaries, and safety you may never have received — while fighting to protect them from the very patterns you're still healing from.

This section is here for the cycle-breakers. For those silently panicking when the in-laws overstep, when your partner freezes, or when your child asks why someone treats you with such disregard. This is for the parent who's torn between wanting to keep the peace and wanting to raise a child who never confuses love with control.

You don't have to replicate the damage to stay in the family. And you don't have to burn everything down to be a protector. You just need tools — and the self-trust to use them. Let's reclaim your role as the safe base your child deserves.

Making Sense Of It
Modeling Secure Attachment in the Presence of Dysfunction

Children notice everything, even when we think they aren't looking. And they don't just notice actions — they feel them. The subtle tension in your jaw when a parent criticizes you, the quiet sigh when your spouse defends that behavior, the moments you swallow your words to keep the peace — all of this lands in their bodies, not just their minds. They are quietly learning what it means to be safe, seen, and respected — or not.

From an attachment perspective, children rely on you to map their emotional world. They are constantly asking: What is normal? What feels safe? What does love feel like? When they see you minimize harm, silence your feelings, or bend repeatedly to protect someone else's ego, they may internalize the message that survival in relationships requires self-betrayal. That the cost of belonging is muting your needs, hiding your truth, or tolerating disrespect. These subtle lessons can shape their own boundaries, self-esteem, and even the way they navigate relationships well into adulthood.

But the reverse is just as powerful. Children learn even more from the ways we demonstrate courage, resilience, and integrity than they do from our words. When you hold boundaries calmly, disengage from manipulative patterns, or express your truth with clarity — even when it's uncomfortable for others — you give them a living model of self-respect. You show them that it's possible to care for others without erasing yourself. That love doesn't require submission. That disagreement doesn't have to feel like danger. And that standing firm in your values can coexist with compassion.

Making Sense Of It

Modeling Secure Attachment in the Presence of Dysfunction

Anthropologically, families have always been the first classrooms for social learning. Across cultures, children observe not just behavior but relational hierarchies, emotional coping strategies, and power dynamics. They learn early who is allowed to speak, who is protected, and who bears the weight of harmony. In households where adults prioritize external appearances over emotional truth, children can grow up assuming that self-silencing is normal. Conversely, when they see caregivers navigating conflict with calm authority, they internalize a model for healthy autonomy, emotional regulation, and respect for boundaries — lessons that ripple far beyond family life.

Parenting in these spaces isn't about shielding children from all dysfunction — that's often impossible. It's about giving them a map for what repair, respect, and resilience look like in real life. When you demonstrate that feelings can be expressed safely, that conflict can be navigated without fear, and that personal boundaries are not just acceptable but essential, you are giving them a blueprint for emotional health that no one else can. You don't need perfection. You need presence, clarity, and alignment between your actions and your values. That is the inheritance that shapes them far more than words alone ever could.

What are you most afraid your children will absorb from watching this family dynamic?

Get honest. Are you modeling silence, fear, resentment, performance? What do you want them to really learn instead?

What are you most afraid your children will absorb from watching this family dynamic?

In what ways have you tried to shield your kids from the in-laws — and at what cost to your own well-being?

Sometimes we overcompensate to protect them, but end up abandoning ourselves. Where are you holding too much?

In what ways have you tried to shield your kids from the in-laws — and at what cost to your own well-being?

What would it look like to protect your child without apologizing for it?

Imagine you no longer needed anyone's permission to parent the way you know is right. What would shift?

What would it look like to protect your child without apologizing for it?

If your child came to you as an adult, describing the dynamic you're living in now — what would you want them to do?

This reversal can be powerful. What advice would you give them about boundaries, loyalty, and emotional health?

If your child came to you as an adult, describing the dynamic you're living in now — what would you want them to do?

What family myths or "rules" are you ready to break so your child doesn't inherit them?

Examples might include: "Respect your elders no matter what", "Keep the peace at all costs", or "Don't rock the boat." Which ones stop here?

What family myths or "rules" are you ready to break so your child doesn't inherit them?

How do you want your children to describe your courage, parenting, and protection — 20 years from now?

Write it as if they were telling someone else: "My parent taught me..." Let your future legacy guide your present actions.

How do you want your children to describe your courage, parenting, and protection — 20 years from now?

TRACING THE TRUTH

THE RIPPLE EFFECT MAP

Every choice you make around boundaries sends ripples your children feel, even if they don't say anything. This exercise helps you visualize that impact so you can make conscious decisions.

Why it helps:
Visualizing your influence shows that modeling healthy boundaries isn't abstract — it's tangible. It highlights what your children are actually learning and gives you a roadmap to consciously shape those lessons.

Draw a circle in the center of a page and write: "My Actions Around Boundaries."
From that circle, draw lines outward like rays or ripples. At the end of each line, write an effect on your child: emotional cues they absorb (stress, anxiety, calm), lessons they learn (what is acceptable, what is safe, what love looks like), or behavioral modeling (conflict navigation, self-respect, people-pleasing).
Add a second layer of ripples for long-term lessons you hope they internalize — resilience, autonomy, self-worth.

Reflect in writing: "Which ripples am I intentionally creating? Which do I want to shift?"

TRACING THE TRUTH

THE RIPPLE EFFECT MAP

TRACING THE TRUTH

THE RIPPLE EFFECT MAP

Reflection:

TRACING THE TRUTH

FUTURE YOU LETTER TO YOUR CHILD

This narrative exercise strengthens the connection between your values and your parenting, giving you clarity on what you want your children to internalize.

Why it helps:
Writing to the future self or child creates an emotional blueprint. It reinforces internal alignment between your actions and your values, while giving your child (and yourself) a tangible model for healthy self-respect and emotional resilience.

Imagine your child ten or fifteen years from now. Picture them navigating relationships, conflict, and their own boundaries.
Write a letter from your present self to that future child, sharing the lessons you hope they carry from how you handled toxic dynamics. For example:
"I hope you remember that it's okay to say no without guilt."
"I hope you saw me honor my feelings and not let fear silence my voice."
"I hope you learned that love doesn't require giving up your self-respect."
Include reflections on what boundaries you want them to witness, even in difficult family situations.
End the letter with a sentence reinforcing self-worth: "I am teaching you through my choices that your feelings matter, and your voice deserves to be heard."

TRACING THE TRUTH

FUTURE YOU LETTER TO YOUR CHILD

TRACING THE TRUTH

FUTURE YOU LETTER TO YOUR CHILD

TRACING THE TRUTH

FUTURE YOU LETTER TO YOUR CHILD

ACTION

SAFE SPACE SCAN

When our mind races with worry or panic, it often ignores the present and imagines danger that isn't real. This simple room scan draws your attention to concrete details, giving your nervous system proof of safety. Naming what's around you slows your thoughts, helps you orient to the present, and reminds your body: I'm here, I'm safe enough, and I can move from here with calm.

Find a quiet spot and take a few steady breaths.

Start at 100 and subtract 5s (or 7 if you prefer) each time: 100, 95, 90... and so on.

Notice when your mind drifts — it will. When it does, gently bring your focus back to the numbers without judgment.

Continue for 2–3 minutes or until your thoughts feel steadier.

ACTION

COOL & RESET

Our nervous system reacts to temperature in ways that can quickly shift arousal. Cool sensations on the face or neck signal the body that danger is passing, helping to calm adrenaline and stress. Spending just a minute noticing the change gives your mind a break from racing thoughts and brings your body into a calmer state — a small but powerful way to regain presence and control.

Find a safe source of cool — a cold pack, splash of water, or even holding something cool in your hands.

Bring it gently to your face or neck. Focus on the sensation for about 60 seconds.

Notice the temperature, the pressure, the way your skin responds, and let your breathing follow the rhythm of the sensation.

SECTION TEN

Reclaiming Your Inner Authority

Few things are more disorienting than feeling like your own sense of safety and truth has been hijacked by someone else's family dynamics. When in-laws dominate the narrative, and your partner can't or won't intervene, it can leave you questioning yourself: "Am I overreacting? Is this really a problem? Why can't I just feel safe?"

This section is for the person whispering, "How do I trust myself when everyone else seems louder, stronger, or more in control?"

We're not here to shame your partner — their inaction often comes from fear, old loyalties, or family scripts they've inherited. This isn't about blaming anyone. It's about reconnecting with your own inner authority, reclaiming clarity, and listening to the voice inside that knows what safety, respect, and boundaries feel like — whether or not anyone else joins you. Because when you reclaim your internal compass, you stop depending on others to validate your reality. And when one person in the system gets clear, it can begin to shift everything.

Making Sense Of It
Reconnecting to Your Inner Compass

When your boundaries are repeatedly ignored, dismissed, or overrun, it's natural to start questioning your own perceptions. That doubt isn't a flaw — it's your nervous system responding to chronic relational stress. In family systems dominated by power struggles, loyalty obligations, or subtle manipulation, your instincts can be muted, overridden, or conditioned to defer. You learn to prioritize harmony over clarity, appeasement over truth. Over time, this internal conditioning can feel like a fog: you sense something is off, but you struggle to trust yourself to name it, let alone act on it.

Humans are wired to orient themselves socially. Anthropological studies show that from early childhood, people calibrate their sense of safety to authority figures, elders, and social hierarchies. In emotionally fused or rigid families, dissent or self-assertion is often met with withdrawal, punishment, or subtle shaming. The result is a nervous system that becomes hyper-aware of others' reactions and under-tuned to your own truth. That doesn't vanish when you leave home; it follows you into adult relationships, especially when in-laws or extended family dynamics are toxic. Your internal compass has been shaped by survival, not by choice.

The good news is that your inner authority can be rebuilt. Trauma-informed research and somatic psychology show that consistent attention to bodily sensations, emotional signals, and internal truths gradually restores trust in your own judgment. Your gut responses, your tense shoulders, the tightness in your chest when something feels wrong — these aren't weaknesses or overreactions.

Making Sense Of It
Reconnecting to Your Inner Compass

They are your body communicating clearly, signaling what matters to you. Listening to them, rather than silencing them, is the first step toward reclaiming power.

Reconnecting to yourself also involves disentangling your truth from others' expectations. When you start identifying which feelings and instincts belong to you — versus what has been imposed by family, culture, or obligation — decision-making becomes more confident. You can distinguish between fear-driven reactions and informed, values-aligned choices. You stop depending on external validation and begin to trust that your reality matters, that your voice matters, and that your boundaries are not negotiable.

This practice doesn't happen overnight. It is a daily reclaiming of presence, clarity, and authority. Each time you honor your internal compass, you strengthen a neural and emotional pathway that had been dormant, teaching your body and mind that you can survive, thrive, and make choices anchored in your own truth. Reclaiming your inner authority doesn't just protect you from toxic dynamics — it rewires how you approach all relationships, giving you the confidence to move through life with your own internal guidance system intact.

What is the specific moment you felt most unprotected by your partner?

Describe the event clearly, including what was said, done, and what you needed but didn't get. Let the truth surface without minimizing.

What is the specific moment you felt most unprotected by your partner?

What did that moment tell you about your partner's unresolved loyalty binds?

Look for patterns. Did they freeze, deflect, make excuses, or change the subject? What might they be protecting — their parents' image, or their own safety?

What did that moment tell you about your partner's unresolved loyalty binds?

Where are you overfunctioning to compensate for their underfunctioning?

Are you the only one setting boundaries, taking emotional risks, or dealing with the fallout? What toll is that taking on your nervous system?

Where are you overfunctioning to compensate for their underfunctioning?

What have you been silently hoping your partner would finally do?

Give yourself permission to name the longing — even if it's painful. "I wish they would just say ___" or "I need them to finally choose ___."

What have you been silently hoping your partner would finally do?

What would alignment — not perfection — look like in this partnership?

Perfection isn't the goal. But what minimums do you need for this relationship to feel safe and collaborative?

What would alignment — not perfection — look like in this partnership?

How are you making yourself small to keep this relationship tolerable?

Where are you biting your tongue, dismissing your needs, or stuffing down rage? What would it feel like to stop doing that?

How are you making yourself small to keep this relationship tolerable?

TRACING THE TRUTH

PATHWAY DIAGRAM — CHOICES & OUTCOMES

Every time you interact with toxic dynamics, you're making choices — some aligned with your truth, others driven by fear or conditioning. This exercise helps you visualize those choices and their consequences, so you can start making empowered decisions in real time.

Why it helps:
Abuse thrives on confusion. When you can clearly see the difference between what happened and the story you tell about it, you interrupt the cycle of self-doubt and emotional hijacking. This practice restores some of your power — because you can't always change your co-parent's behavior, but you can reclaim how you make sense of it.

- **On the next page**, use the three arrows branching downward from the circle, each representing a possible response:
- **Option 1: Fear-driven / conditioned** — what your survival reflex might do automatically (e.g., people-pleasing, silence, fawning).
- **Option 2: Passive / avoidant** — what you might do to "keep peace" or minimize conflict.
- **Option 3: Empowered / aligned with your truth** — how you would respond if you trusted your inner authority (e.g., calm boundary-setting, clear language, disengagement).
- **At the end of each branch, draw a smaller circle and label it:** "Outcome / Feeling". Reflect on the likely consequences of each choice, including emotional, relational, and somatic impacts.
- **Optional: Add a fourth branch for creative alternative responses that haven't occurred to you yet** — what might you try next time?

TRACING THE TRUTH

PATHWAY DIAGRAM — CHOICES & OUTCOMES

TRACING THE TRUTH

PATHWAY DIAGRAM — CHOICES & OUTCOMES

Reflect in writing: Which pathways feel easiest to take? Which feel safest for your nervous system? Which align with your values and your internal compass?

ACTION

EMOTION PAUSE & SHIFT

Emotions are powerful signals, but they don't always reflect the full truth of a situation. Sometimes anger, fear, or shame pushes us toward behaviors that make things worse—reacting sharply, withdrawing, or avoiding. Opposite Action gives you a way to step out of automatic emotional reactions and act in a way that aligns with your values and long-term well-being. By pausing, checking if the emotion is justified, and responding intentionally in the opposite direction, you teach your mind and body that you can handle emotions without letting them control you. Over time, this reduces emotional reactivity and strengthens self-trust.

Name the emotion and urge.
Example: Anger → yelling at someone.

Check the facts.
Is the intensity of the emotion justified by what actually happened, or is it amplified by past patterns, assumptions, or stress?

Choose the opposite behavior.
Act in a way that's constructive, compassionate, or gentle.
Example: Use a calm tone, approach the person respectfully, or step away for a mindful pause.

Stay with the emotion.
Continue the opposite behavior until the intensity drops by about half. Notice how your body and mind respond differently.

> ACTION

NERVOUS SYSTEM RESET

Sometimes your body gets stuck in high alert—heart racing, muscles tight, mind spiraling—and it's hard to think or respond clearly. TIP Skills target the physiology directly, calming your nervous system so your emotions have space to settle. Using temperature, movement, and breathing strategically helps you interrupt the stress response, release adrenaline, and regain a sense of control. This isn't about ignoring feelings—it's about resetting your body so you can respond thoughtfully instead of reacting out of overwhelm.

  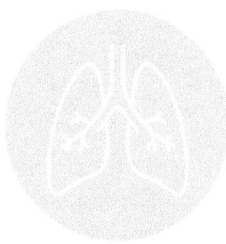 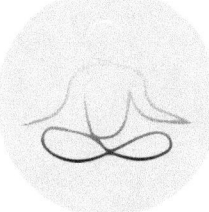

T = TEMPERATURE

Splash cool water on your face or neck, or use a cold pack. This signals your body that it's safe to downshift.

I = INTENSE EXERCISE

Create several posts of the same type at once, schedule them using an app, and upload them so they are available at the right time

P = PACED BREATHING

You can save time by copying and pasting the CTA into your posts instead of writing it out again every time

P = PROGRESSIVE MUSCLE RELAXATION

Create some posts with a frame around your branding image. You can reuse the same image after at least 9 posts but change the brand colour for a different look

SECTION ELEVEN

Staying, Leaving, or Going Low Contact – Choosing Peace Over Obligation

There comes a point when you've tried every angle — speaking gently, setting boundaries, enduring in silence, even sacrificing parts of yourself for the sake of peace. And still, nothing changes. That's when the question shifts from "How do I make this work?" to "Is this working for me at all?"

This section is for the person standing at the edge, wondering if the cost of connection has become too high.

Whether you're considering limited contact, full estrangement, or simply refusing to keep abandoning yourself to preserve a broken dynamic, this chapter will walk you through it with clarity and care.

These decisions are never simple. Grief and guilt will likely surface. So will freedom and relief. You are allowed to choose yourself — not out of spite, but out of wisdom. This is about choosing peace over performance, authenticity over obligation, and a life that no longer requires you to shrink to survive.

Making Sense Of It
Trauma Loyalty and Choosing Yourself

Remaining in toxic dynamics out of guilt, fear, or obligation often isn't just a choice — it's a deep, unconscious pattern called trauma loyalty. This is the belief that enduring pain is proof of love, or that bending yourself to fit someone else's expectations is necessary to stay safe, accepted, or connected. Trauma loyalty is wired into your nervous system long before you could name it: when caregivers were unpredictable, manipulative, or dismissive, you learned to contort yourself to preserve the bond. Survival meant giving up pieces of yourself.

As adults, these old scripts are triggered again when in-laws, partners, or extended family mirror familiar dynamics. Suddenly, the same thought loops appear: "Maybe if I try harder, maybe if I explain again, maybe if I forgive, they'll change." Your body remembers the patterns, your mind rationalizes, and your heart hopes — all while quietly paying a price in energy, peace, and clarity. Anthropologically, humans are wired to maintain social cohesion; in-group survival often trumped personal safety in our evolutionary past. Trauma loyalty is the modern echo of that survival instinct.

Healing begins with a radical reframing: you are not obligated to be loyal to pain just because it wears a family name. Choosing low contact, no contact, or firm distance is not betrayal — it is protection. It is an act of courage, self-respect, and nervous system regulation. It communicates to yourself and your body that your wellbeing matters, that your voice matters, and that you get to define the rules of connection in your life. This is a critical step in trauma recovery. The people who respect your boundaries will rise to meet them; those who cannot are not worth the cost of your peace.

What are you currently tolerating in this dynamic that goes against your values, wellbeing, or peace?

Write without justification. Get honest about what you've allowed and how it's harming you — emotionally, physically, relationally.

What are you currently tolerating in this dynamic that goes against your values, wellbeing, or peace?

What beliefs keep you feeling trapped in this relationship or system?

Are you afraid of being the bad guy? Of causing pain? Of family backlash? Trace the fears to their origins — are they yours, or inherited?

What beliefs keep you feeling trapped in this relationship or system?

What would change in your life — practically and emotionally — if you chose low contact, no contact, or a firm boundary?

Imagine the grief and the relief. The silence and the space. Let both possibilities exist.

What would change in your life — practically and emotionally — if you chose low contact, no contact, or a firm boundary?

If your inner child could decide, what would they want you to do?

Return to that younger part of you. What would they beg you to stop enduring? What kind of safety would they choose?

If your inner child could decide, what would they want you to do?

What version of peace are you ready to claim?

Define peace your way. Is it quiet? Is it strong boundaries? Is it no longer having to rehearse conversations in your head?

What version of peace are you ready to claim?

Who would be upset by your choice — and why does their disappointment feel dangerous?

Name the people. Then ask: Is it actually dangerous, or just emotionally charged? What are you afraid will happen — and what would actually happen?

Who would be upset by your choice — and why does their disappointment feel dangerous?

TRACING THE TRUTH

THE LOYALTY WEB

Trauma loyalty often feels invisible — like invisible strings connecting you to people, expectations, and obligations that don't serve you. This exercise helps you see the web so you can decide where to cut, soften, or reinforce connections.

Why it helps:
By externalizing invisible obligations, you can literally see where trauma loyalty is holding you back. It transforms abstract feelings of guilt into actionable insight, helping you start consciously managing who and what deserves your energy.

Look at the next page. Around you, draw smaller circles for all the people, dynamics, or roles you feel obligated to due to trauma loyalty (family members, in-laws, traditions, "keeping peace," etc.).
Connect yourself to each circle with lines representing the strength of obligation / guilt (thicker lines = stronger loyalty pressure).
For each line, write a short note: "Why do I feel obligated?" and "What does it cost me?"

Use color or markers to highlight:
Lines you want to loosen (lower contact, say no)
Lines you want to cut completely
Lines that are healthy and mutual

TRACING THE TRUTH

THE LOYALTY WEB

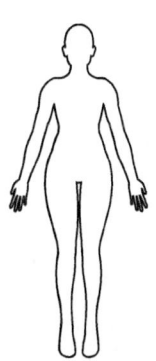

ACTION

RESILIENCE LOG

When life feels heavy, it's easy to overlook all the ways you're managing, showing up, or making a difference—especially when old beliefs tell you you're not enough. This log helps you notice the small but real evidence of your resilience, care, and competence each day. Recording these moments rewires your focus from what went wrong to what actually happened, giving your mind proof that you are capable, contributing, and connected. Ending with a short reflection ties it all together, reinforcing a more balanced and compassionate view of yourself.

Record daily moments where you are:

   Coping with a challenge (e.g., managing a tense conversation, taking a pause before reacting).
   Contributing or helping (e.g., supporting a friend, completing a task, showing up for someone).
   Connecting (e.g., reaching out to someone, expressing your feelings, listening fully).

End each entry with a reflection:
"What this says about me is ___." Example: "I am capable of handling difficult moments with care."

Review weekly. Notice patterns of strength, resilience, and connection that you might normally overlook.

Day	Coping with a challenge	Contributing or helping	Connecting	Reflection

ACTION

RESILIENCE LOG

Day	Coping with a challenge	Contributing or helping	Connecting	Reflection

274

SECTION TWELVE

Parenting in the Eye of the Storm

Raising children while navigating toxic in-law dynamics can feel like walking a tightrope over a stormy sea. Every decision, every interaction, carries weight — not just for you, but for the little minds and hearts watching, learning, and absorbing every subtle cue. The stress, the tension, the quiet dread of what your child might witness — it's all real, and it's heavy.

Maybe you catch yourself second-guessing every boundary: "If I say no, will I be the villain? If I let it slide, am I teaching them it's okay to tolerate harm?" Maybe you're exhausted from constantly negotiating between your own triggers and the family pressures that never seem to let up. That tension can feel endless, and yet, your awareness is the first step toward change.

Here's the truth: your children don't inherit your pain automatically. They inherit what you model. When you choose clarity over guilt, boundaries over appeasement, and self-respect over silent endurance, you are giving them a roadmap for safety, emotional literacy, and strength. You get to be the parent you needed, showing them that love doesn't come at the cost of integrity. This work is profound.

Making Sense Of It
Breaking the Generational Trauma Loop

Children are wired to observe and absorb far more than we often realize. From the earliest months, they track emotional tone, tension, and relational patterns, internalizing subtle cues about safety, trust, and what it means to be seen. When toxic in-law dynamics intrude — through criticism, boundary violations, or emotional manipulation — children are not passive witnesses. They are learning, moment by moment, what is normal, what is permissible, and what they might need to sacrifice to keep relationships intact.

From an attachment perspective, your child looks to you as the emotional barometer: your responses teach them how the world works. If you shrink, people-please, or suppress discomfort to avoid conflict, they may unconsciously adopt those same patterns. Anthropologically, humans evolved to prioritize in-group cohesion, often at the expense of personal safety — a survival mechanism that can ripple through family systems. In modern contexts, children inherit this tension as internalized relational rules, even if the original family context is gone.

But there is profound opportunity here. Your nervous system, your choices, and your presence become teaching tools. When you model calm, assertive boundaries and name emotional truths appropriately, you give your children a blueprint for self-respect, emotional literacy, and resilience. They learn that discomfort can exist without surrendering integrity, that conflict can be managed without fear, and that love is never conditional on self-abandonment.

Making Sense Of It
Breaking the Generational Trauma Loop

This isn't about perfection. It's about alignment and visibility: showing up as a parent who honors your inner compass, who navigates relational complexity with integrity, and who demonstrates that safety and care can coexist even in difficult circumstances. The ripple effect of these lessons is enormous — children internalize not just what to do, but what is possible: a life where respect, boundaries, and love are not mutually exclusive.

Ultimately, parenting through toxic in-law dynamics is transformational. It rewires inherited trauma, interrupts intergenerational patterns, and allows your child to inherit not your wounds, but your courage and clarity. Your presence, your modeling, and your steady commitment to integrity are among the most radical acts of healing you can perform — for both yourself and the next generation.

What do I want my children to believe about family, love, and boundaries — based on what they see from me?

Get specific. Do you want them to know love isn't conditional? That they can say no? That they're allowed to walk away from what hurts?

What do I want my children to believe about family, love, and boundaries — based on what they see from me?

What toxic dynamics have I tolerated or explained away in front of my children? Why did I feel I had to?

Explore where you've silenced yourself "for the kids," and what unspoken messages may have been passed down.

What toxic dynamics have I tolerated or explained away in front of my children? Why did I feel I had to?

In what ways am I still parenting from a place of fear or reactivity?

Notice where your inner child is in the driver's seat — trying to do the opposite of what you grew up with, but from a place of panic instead of calm clarity.

In what ways am I still parenting from a place of fear or reactivity?

What does protection look like, in practice — not just theory — when it comes to my kids and toxic relatives?

Define it. Is it supervised visits? Is it cutting off contact? Is it being honest with your child in an age-appropriate way?

What does protection look like, in practice — not just theory — when it comes to my kids and toxic relatives?

What parts of me still need permission to become the protective parent I never had?

Let that inner child speak. What do they need to feel safe enough to say, "No more"?

What parts of me still need permission to become the protective parent I never had?

If I trusted myself completely as a parent, what decisions would I make differently?

Set aside the guilt, the noise, the pressure. What would shift if you believed you were already enough?

If I trusted myself completely as a parent, what decisions would I make differently?

TRACING THE TRUTH

Emotional Ripple Map

Your emotions and choices as a parent ripple outward, shaping your child's nervous system and their understanding of relationships. This exercise helps you visualize and track those ripples so you can see the real impact of your presence.

Why it helps:
Visualizing the impact of your actions makes abstract concepts concrete. It helps you see the tangible ways your modeling teaches resilience, boundaries, and self-respect — and it reinforces the power you already have as a parent, even in difficult dynamics.

On the next page, draw a small circle in the center labeled "Me / My Choices."
Around that circle, draw larger concentric rings representing your child's emotional world, their behaviors, and their perception of relationships.
For each ring, note specific ways your choices influence them — e.g., boundary-setting, calm conflict navigation, emotional honesty, self-care, or reactions to toxic relatives.
Reflect: Which ripples are positive? Which areas feel shaky or inconsistent? Where can you intentionally create steadier, safer ripples?

Optional: Use different colors to represent feelings like calm, fear, tension, or joy to make the map more dynamic.

TRACING THE TRUTH

Emotional Ripple Map

293

ACTION

THE TRIGGER MAP

When you react automatically, it often feels like there's no pause between what happens and how you respond. This exercise helps you slow things down and see the chain of events clearly—what triggered the feeling, the thought that popped up, the urge, and what actually happened. Once you can see it all laid out, you can spot the point where you can intervene next time. That small pause is enough to change the outcome, give yourself more control, and break patterns that have been running on autopilot.

Map the chain: Write down each step in order

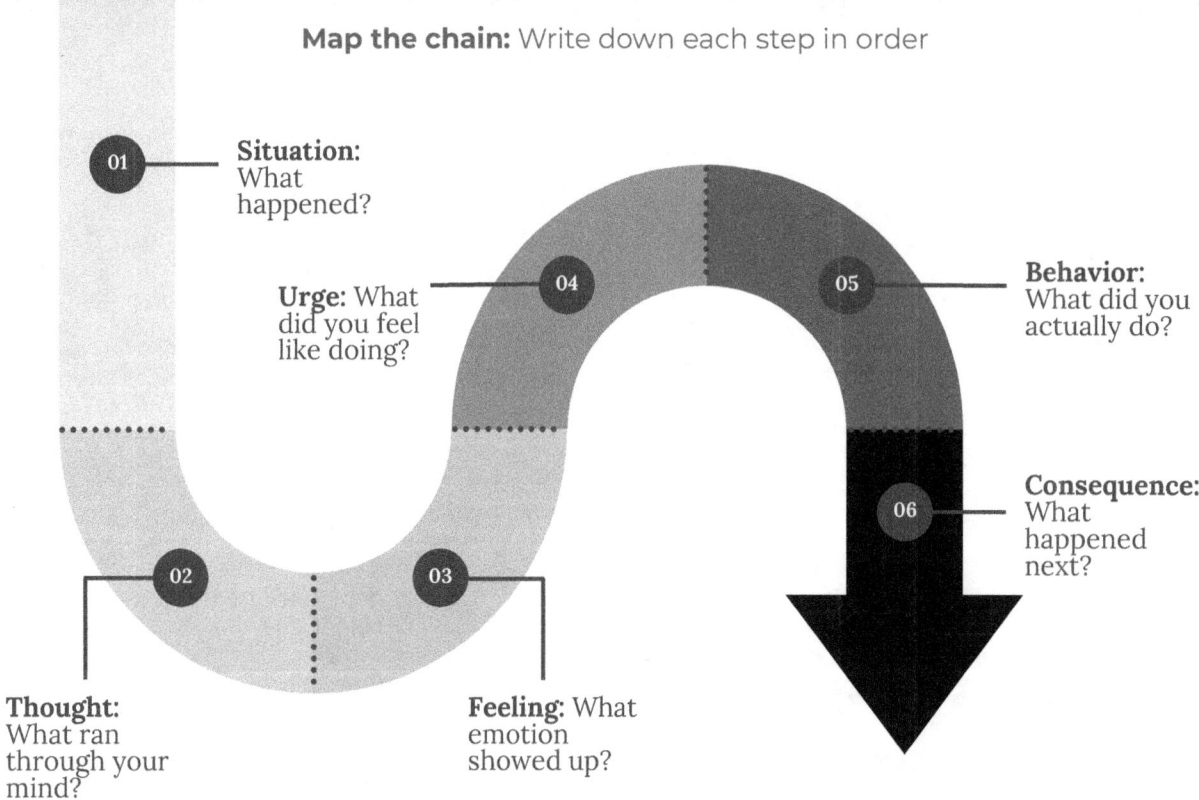

01 **Situation:** What happened?

02 **Thought:** What ran through your mind?

03 **Feeling:** What emotion showed up?

04 **Urge:** What did you feel like doing?

05 **Behavior:** What did you actually do?

06 **Consequence:** What happened next?

Circle your change point. Look at the chain and find the first step where you could intervene next time.

Plan one interruption. Pick a tool or skill to use—like a short breathing exercise, a script you can say, or a grounding move—to pause the chain and respond differently.

ACTION

CLIMBING DOWN

When your mind hits you with a brutal thought—like "I always mess up"—it can feel impossible to jump straight to a positive or kind belief. Your brain just won't buy it. This exercise gives you a middle ground. By writing the harsh thought at the top and gradually stepping down to gentler, more realistic versions, you give yourself space to find a statement that actually feels believable. Even if it's not perfect, that 70% believable thought is enough to lower the intensity and guide you toward calmer choices today.

Write the harsh thought at the top rung. (e.g., "I always mess up.")
Step down slowly. Each rung is a slightly softer, more balanced version of the thought.
  "I mess up sometimes, but not always."
  "Everyone makes mistakes. Mine don't erase the things I do well."
  "I can learn from this and try again."
Pick the rung that feels about 70% true. You don't have to land at the bottom. Just stop where it feels believable.
Act from that rung. Let today's choices come from this steadier, more grounded statement.

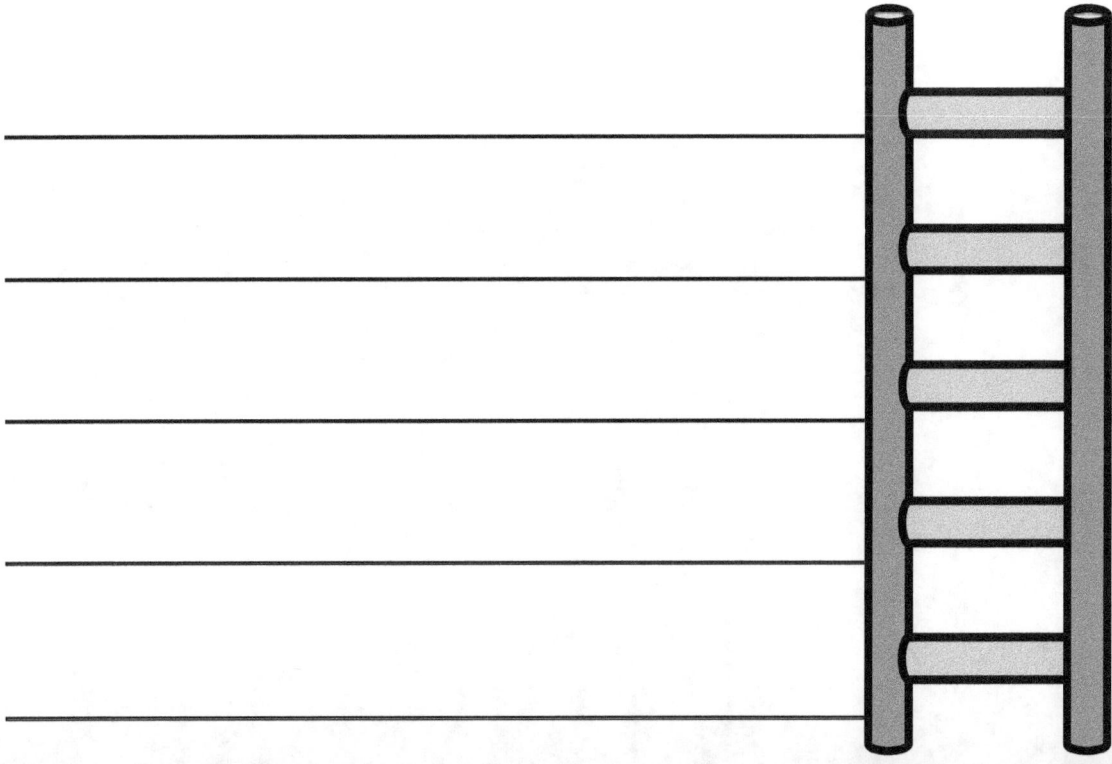

SECTION THIRTEEN

Letting Go of the Fantasy – Grieving the Relationship You Wished They Could Be

No one tells you how much grief is tangled up in the anger. Underneath the frustration, the tension, the emotional labor — there's a quiet, aching sorrow: they were supposed to be different.

You might've longed for a second parent figure, a mentor, a welcoming embrace. Someone to celebrate holidays with, spoil your kids, or simply treat you with kindness. Instead, you got control, cruelty, judgment, or absence. And even if you've accepted it logically, your heart may still be holding on to a version of them that never existed — but should have.

This section is about naming that grief. Letting it be real. Letting it hurt — not because you're weak, but because your capacity for love runs deep.

Releasing the fantasy doesn't mean you're giving up hope. It means you're setting your heart free from false promises. You deserve to grieve what wasn't — so you can finally breathe in what is.

Making Sense Of It
Mourning What Was Never Fully Yours

Some of the heaviest grief is the kind that has no clear beginning or end — grief for someone who is physically present but emotionally absent, someone who cannot meet you where you need them to be. In trauma work, this is called ambiguous grief: mourning what was never fully alive, yet profoundly real. It's the ache for connection that keeps slipping through your fingers, heartbreak without closure, and longing that never seems to resolve.

When toxic family dynamics are involved, this grief can feel endless. Every holiday, every attempt at conversation, every act of "trying one more time" can reopen the wound. Anthropologically, humans are wired to seek reciprocity in relationships — when it's absent, the nervous system flags it as danger, triggering cycles of hope, disappointment, and emotional hypervigilance. This is why you may find yourself stuck in loops of yearning and regret, even when your rational mind knows the situation is unlikely to change. Letting go of the fantasy doesn't mean giving up on love or hope. It means redirecting your care toward yourself, reclaiming energy that's been trapped in invisible contracts of expectation. It's about cultivating safety in your own nervous system, creating rituals, boundaries, and support that nurture your wellbeing rather than keep you tethered to unmet needs. Psychologically, this is powerful: it rewires attachment patterns, strengthens emotional resilience, and breaks the invisible inheritance of relational trauma.

Culturally and socially, many of us are taught that family loyalty or endurance is sacred — that grief without closure is shameful, and self-protection is selfish. In reality, honoring your limits and prioritizing your emotional life is radical self-care, one of the most loving acts you can do for yourself and your children. Each time you step out of hope-for-the-unavailable loops, you give yourself permission to live fully, with clarity, integrity, and freedom. This is not abandonment — it is presence, strength, and the reclamation of life you deserve, on your terms.

What did I hope this relationship would be — before I knew who they really were?

Write about the original dream. The version of them you once wished for. What did you long to receive?

What did I hope this relationship would be — before I knew who they really were?

How have I kept trying to earn or recreate that fantasy, even in small ways?

Look at the emotional effort — the overexplaining, the holiday compromises, the hope you keep quietly reviving.

How have I kept trying to earn or recreate that fantasy, even in small ways?

What do I lose when I keep holding on to who they "should have been"?

Time? Peace? Energy? Self-trust? Identify the cost of clinging to an ideal they've never lived up to.

What do I lose when I keep holding on to who they "should have been"?

What do I feel when I imagine letting the fantasy go — sadness, relief, fear?

Let the grief speak honestly. You don't have to force positivity. Grief is part of growing up emotionally.

What do I feel when I imagine letting the fantasy go — sadness, relief, fear?

What do I still need to hear, feel, or say to get closure — even if I never get it from them?

Imagine speaking it aloud. Write the unspoken sentence. It may sound like: "You never saw me. And that hurt."

What do I still need to hear, feel, or say to get closure —
even if I never get it from them?

Who am I without the dream of fixing this relationship?

If you let that weight go — the fantasy, the pressure — what becomes possible in your life?

Who am I without the dream of fixing this relationship?

TRACING THE TRUTH

THE GRIEF LETTER

Sometimes the grief we carry isn't just for what happened — it's for what we imagined could be, the version of someone we wished existed. Writing to that imagined version allows you to honor your pain, acknowledge your unmet needs, and begin reclaiming your emotional energy.

Why it helps:
This exercise externalizes unresolved hope and grief, providing a safe container to express emotions that might otherwise stay trapped in the body or mind. The combination of narrative processing and somatic release interrupts the trauma loop, strengthens emotional clarity, and reinforces your agency — you are not waiting for them anymore; you are choosing yourself.

Think of the version of them you wished existed — the kind, safe, emotionally present person.
Write a letter to that version, including:
What you needed from them
What you hoped for
What it cost you to keep hoping
End the letter with a clear goodbye. For example:
"I wanted you to be real. I can't keep waiting. I choose my own peace."

Optional: Tear, fold, or otherwise remove the letter to mark the ending of that hope.

TRACING THE TRUTH

THE GRIEF LETTER

TRACING THE TRUTH

THE GRIEF LETTER

TRACING THE TRUTH

THE GRIEF LETTER

ACTION

THE CONFIDENCE LADDER

Some moments in life trigger intense fear, anxiety, or discomfort—like standing up for yourself, expressing a difficult emotion, or setting a boundary. When we avoid these moments, the fear grows and feels bigger than it really is. A graded exposure plan helps you face these challenges slowly and safely. By breaking a difficult situation into small, manageable steps, practicing until the intensity eases, and moving up gradually, you build confidence and prove to yourself that you can handle tough moments without being overwhelmed. Over time, the things that once felt impossible feel doable.

Identify a fear or difficult situation. This could be sharing your feelings, saying no, or speaking your truth.

Fill out the 10 step ladder. 0 = completely safe, 10 = maximum fear. Break the situation into small steps that feel increasingly challenging.

Example: 3 = briefly stating a need in your mind, 5 = saying it in a low-stakes moment, 7 = expressing it fully in a more challenging situation.

Start low. Practice the step until the fear noticeably decreases.

Move up one step at a time. No rushing, no pressure—just steady, repeated practice.

Reflect on progress. Each rung is proof that you can handle difficult moments safely, building trust in yourself and your ability to respond calmly.

ACTION

THE CONFIDENCE LADDER

SECTION FOURTEEN

Staying, Leaving, or Detaching – Making the Right Choice for You

At some point, we all reach a crossroads. Maybe you've tried everything. Maybe you're exhausted. Or maybe you're just starting to realize that peace doesn't come from them changing — it comes from you deciding what you need.

This final section is about choice — not the kind shaped by guilt or pressure, but the kind that's rooted in clarity, safety, and self-trust. Whether you decide to stay in some form of contact, go fully no-contact, or emotionally detach while remaining involved (for your partner, kids, or culture), this work is about giving yourself permission.

There's no one right answer — only what's most aligned with your nervous system, your values, and your future. Some people need distance to heal. Others need boundaries that hold. And some need a full goodbye.
Whatever you choose, you're not weak. You're not selfish. You're reclaiming your right to live in peace — without asking anyone else for permission.

Making Sense Of It
Choosing Your Path with Clarity

At some point, you reach a threshold where exhaustion meets clarity — the moment you realize that waiting for others to change is a trap, and that peace is a decision you get to make for yourself. In family systems and trauma work, this is often called differentiation of self: the ability to remain connected to others without losing your own center. It's about being grounded in your values, aware of your boundaries, and emotionally intact, even when those around you are chaotic, controlling, or unavailable.

Toxic in-law dynamics often force a false dichotomy: stay and sacrifice your needs, or walk away entirely. But real freedom is rarely this binary. Conscious differentiation allows you to create a third path: a stance of internal clarity and emotional detachment, where your choices aren't dictated by fear, guilt, or obligation. You define what interactions are acceptable, what energy you will offer, and where your boundaries will hold — even if the external situation remains the same.

Neuroscience shows that chronic exposure to relational stress hijacks the nervous system, keeping us in fight, flight, freeze, or fawn states. By practicing internal differentiation, you signal to your nervous system that you are safe, even when others are not, reclaiming agency over your emotional responses. You may remain physically present for children, cultural expectations, or shared responsibilities, yet emotionally you are centered — not tethered to chaos, guilt, or manipulation.

This is radical self-trust in action. Freedom doesn't always require leaving; sometimes it is simply knowing you can leave, and choosing your stance from clarity rather than fear. It's the ultimate reclamation of your nervous system, your values, and your right to live in peace. Whatever path you choose — distance, boundaries, or full goodbye — the work lies in aligning your inner world with your needs, not in convincing anyone else to meet you there.

What are the emotional, cultural, or practical reasons I've stayed connected — and are they still valid for me today?

Explore whether your reasons for maintaining contact are still aligned with your values, or driven by fear, habit, or outside pressure.

What are the emotional, cultural, or practical reasons I've stayed connected — and are they still valid for me today?

What am I afraid will happen if I go low-contact, no-contact, or speak my truth?

Let your nervous system speak honestly. Don't push it. Just name the fear. You can soothe it once it's visible.

What am I afraid will happen if I go low-contact, no-contact, or speak my truth?

What would freedom feel like — in my body, in my life, in my home — if I made the decision that was best for me?

Paint the sensory picture. Calm mornings. Uninterrupted parenting. Holidays without dread. Claim it.

What would freedom feel like — in my body, in my life, in my home — if I made the decision that was best for me?

If I could do this without guilt, what would I choose?

Sometimes we know what we want — we just don't give ourselves permission to want it.

> If I could do this without guilt, what would I choose?

What is the cost of staying connected in the way things are now? What am I losing, emotionally or energetically?

Let this be a reckoning. You don't need shame — just truth. You deserve to see the full picture.

What is the cost of staying connected in the way things are now? What am I losing, emotionally or energetically?

What boundaries or choices would protect my peace and dignity, even if I don't go fully no-contact?

Could it be shorter visits? No direct messaging? No access to your children? Get specific.

What boundaries or choices would protect my peace and dignity, even if I don't go fully no-contact?

Who am I allowed to become if I no longer shape my life around their behavior or approval?

This is the question that opens doors. Go deep. Be bold.

Who am I allowed to become if I no longer shape my life around their behavior or approval?

TRACING THE TRUTH

ALIGNMENT CHECK

Your inner clarity is the best guide for what you can tolerate and what you cannot. This exercise links reflection with somatic awareness.

Why it helps:
This exercise connects cognitive decision-making with somatic intuition, helping you distinguish fear-based choices from clarity-based ones. It reinforces self-trust and shows that your nervous system can guide your decisions as effectively as your mind.

Sit quietly and notice how your body reacts to thoughts of staying, limiting, or leaving contact with toxic family members. Where do you feel tension, heaviness, or openness?
Write down each option in your journal. Next to each, note your body's response: tight chest, relaxed shoulders, fluttering stomach, lightness, etc.
Ask yourself: "Which choice feels like integrity in my body? Which choice drains me?"
Circle the option that resonates most with both your values and your nervous system sense of safety.

Close your eyes, take three deep breaths, and visualize yourself acting from that choice — grounded, centered, and supported.

STONEWELL HEALING PRESS

ASSESSMENT

HOW FAR I'VE COME

You've done the work — now let's see where you're at. Take a moment to rate these statements again with honesty and self-compassion. Notice what's shifted, what still feels raw, and what that means for your next steps.

1-10

1. I trust my own perception, even when others try to twist or dismiss my reality.

2. I can set boundaries without being swallowed by guilt, fear, or shame.

3. I value my own peace more than avoiding conflict or keeping others comfortable.

4. I can recognize gaslighting in the moment and hold onto my clarity instead of collapsing into confusion.

5. I notice how stress shows up in my body and respond with care instead of ignoring or pushing through.

6. When my needs or boundaries are dismissed, I can respond in a way that protects my dignity and self-respect.

7. I can sit with hard emotions—anger, grief, fear—without shutting down, exploding, or abandoning myself.

8. When I picture my future relationships, I imagine myself safe, respected, and fully present as my whole self.

Mindset & Identity Shift Reflection

Healing changes the way you see yourself. You might notice you're less reactive in certain moments, more confident speaking up, or simply softer with yourself. This page is about spotting those shifts — the ones that show you're not the same person who started this journey.

In what ways do I see myself differently than when I started?

What beliefs about myself or others are shifting?

How has my sense of hope, strength, or trust evolved?

MOVING FORWARD

ACTION PLAN

This is your personalized roadmap for continuing growth beyond this workbook. Use this space to clarify which skills you'll keep practicing, how you'll notice early warning signs, and what concrete steps you'll take to support yourself. Remember, transformation happens one intentional step at a time.

Skills I will keep practicing regularly

Early warning signs or triggers I'll watch for:

When I notice these signs, here's what I will do:

MOVING FORWARD

ACTION PLAN

This is your personalized roadmap for continuing growth beyond this workbook. Use this space to clarify which skills you'll keep practicing, how you'll notice early warning signs, and what concrete steps you'll take to support yourself. Remember, transformation happens one intentional step at a time.

Ways I can check in with myself to monitor progress (daily, weekly, monthly):	
People or supports I will reach out to if I need encouragement or accountability:	
One commitment I'm making to myself right now:	

RESOURCE LIST

The resources listed here are shared for informational purposes only. While they provide valuable support and tools for mental health, I am not endorsing or guaranteeing the quality, effectiveness, or availability of their services. It's important to explore these options and verify the details directly on their websites to ensure they align with your personal needs.

National Alliance on Mental Illness

www.nami.org

Offers free mental health education, peer support, and a 24/7 helpline.

Insight Timer

www.insighttimer.com

A free meditation app with thousands of guided meditations, music, and talks on mental well-being

Parenting for Mental Health

www.parentingformentalhealth.com

Offers resources, training, and advice on how parents can support their child's mental health, including guides and printable resources

Crisis Text Line

www.crisistextline.org

Offers free, 24/7 text-based support for mental health crises

7 Cups

www.7cups.com

Offers free, anonymous online chat with trained volunteers, as well as paid therapy with licensed professionals.

There's a special kind of grief that comes from being tied to people who never saw you clearly, never respected your boundaries, and maybe never even liked you — but still expected your silence, your performance, your compliance. Maybe they never welcomed you. Maybe they competed with you, disrespected you, tried to control your home, your children, your marriage — or made you question your worth. Whatever their tactics, the weight of surviving a toxic in-law dynamic can leave deep bruises that no one sees. You're not weak for feeling it. You're not overreacting for needing distance. And you're not broken for being affected. Protecting yourself isn't cruelty — it's clarity. Sometimes the hardest grief is mourning the relationship you wished you could have had with them. But healing means giving up the performance, letting go of the hope that they'll suddenly become someone safe, and choosing to show up for yourself instead. You are allowed to live in peace. You are allowed to take up space in your own life. And you don't have to set yourself on fire to keep someone else's fragile ego warm. Let that be the end of the cycle — right here. Right now.

> You don't owe anyone access to your peace, your children, your home, or your emotional well-being just because they're "family." Family is earned. Respect is mutual. And your boundaries don't need to be justified — they just need to be respected.

M. Tourangeau
Stonewell Healing Press

www.ingramcontent.com/pod-product-compliance
Lightning Source LLC
Chambersburg PA
CBHW080834230426
43665CB00021B/2841